For Rene,

And the pursuit of equanimity.

— Polly

Dhammapada

Other books in the
SkyLight Illuminations Series

Bhagavad Gita: Annotated & Explained

The Book of Mormon: Selections Annotated & Explained

The Gospel of Thomas: Annotated & Explained

Hasidic Tales: Annotated & Explained

The Hebrew Prophets: Selections Annotated & Explained

The Hidden Gospel of Matthew: Annotated & Explained

Rumi and Islam: Selections from His Stories, Poems, and Discourses—Annotated & Explained

The Secret Book of John: The Gnostic Gospel—Annotated & Explained

Selections from the Gospel of Sri Ramakrishna: Annotated & Explained

Spiritual Texts on Mary: Annotated & Explained

The Way of a Pilgrim: Annotated & Explained

Zohar: Annotated & Explained

Dhammapada

Annotated & Explained

Annotation by
Jack Maguire

Translation by
Max Müller;
Revised by
Jack Maguire

Foreword by Andrew Harvey

Walking Together, Finding the Way

SKYLIGHT PATHS PUBLISHING
WOODSTOCK, VERMONT

Dhammapada:
Annotated & Explained

2005 Second Printing
2002 First Printing

Library of Congress Cataloging-in-Publication Data

Tipiòtaka. Suttapiòtaka. Khuddakanikåaya. Dhammapada. English.
Dhammapada : annotated & explained/translation by Max Müller ; annotation by Jack Maguire.
p. cm.
ISBN 1-893361-42-X (pbk.)
I. Müller, F. Max (Friedrich Max), 1823–1900. II. Maguire, Jack, 1945– III. Title.
BQ1372.E54 T54 2001
294.3'82322—dc21

2001006103

10 9 8 7 6 5 4 3 2

Manufactured in the United States of America

Cover design: Walter C. Bumford III

Walking Together, Finding the Way
Published by SkyLight Paths Publishing
A Division of LongHill Partners, Inc.
Sunset Farm Offices, Route 4, P.O. Box 237
Woodstock, VT 05091
Tel: (802) 457-4000 Fax: (802) 457-4004
www.skylightpaths.com

All created things are impermanent.
Strive with diligence for your release.

—*The Buddha's last words*

ဓမ္မပဒပါဠိ

၁. ယမကဝဂ္ဂေါ

၁. မနောပုဗ္ဗင်္ဂမာ ဓမ္မာ၊ မနောသေဋ္ဌာ မနောမယာ။
မနသာ စေ ပဒုဋ္ဌေန၊ ဘာသတိ ဝါ ကရောတိ ဝါ။
တတော နံ ဒုက္ခမနွေတိ၊ စက္ကံဝ ဝဟတော ပဒံ။
၂. မနောပုဗ္ဗင်္ဂမာ ဓမ္မာ၊ မနောသေဋ္ဌာ မနောမယာ။
မနသာ စေ ပသန္နေန၊ ဘာသတိ ဝါ ကရောတိ ဝါ။
တတော နံ သုခမနွေတိ၊ ဆာယာဝ အနပါယိနီ။
၃. အက္ကောစ္ဆိ မံ အဝဓိ မံ၊ အဇိနိ မံ အဟာသိ မေ။
ယေ စ တံ ဥပနယှန္တိ၊ ဝေရံ တေသံ န သမ္မတိ။
၄. အက္ကောစ္ဆိ မံ အဝဓိ မံ၊ အဇိနိ မံ အဟာသိ မေ။
ယေ စ တံ နုပနယှန္တိ၊ ဝေရံ တေသူပသမ္မတိ။
၅. န ဟိ ဝေရေန ဝေရာနိ၊ သမ္မန္တီဓ ကုဒါစနံ။
အဝေရေန စ သမ္မန္တိ၊ ဧသ ဓမ္မော သနန္တနော။
၆. ပရေ စ န ဝိဇာနန္တိ၊ မယမေတ္ထ ယမာမသေ။
ယေ စ တတ္ထ ဝိဇာနန္တိ၊ တတော သမ္မန္တိ မေဓဂါ။
၇. သုဘာနုပဿိံ ဝိဟရန္တံ၊ ဣန္ဒြိယေသု အသံဝုတံ။
ဘောဇနမှိ စာမတ္တညုံ၊ ကုသီတံ ဟီနဝီရိယံ။
တံ ဝေ ပသဟတိ မာရော၊ ဝါတော ရုက္ခံဝ ဒုဗ္ဗလံ။
၈. အသုဘာနုပဿိံ ဝိဟရန္တံ၊ ဣန္ဒြိယေသု သုသံဝုတံ။
ဘောဇနမှိ စ မတ္တညုံ၊ သဒ္ဓံ အာရဒ္ဓဝီရိယံ။
တံ ဝေ နပ္ပသဟတိ မာရော၊ ဝါတော သေလံဝ ပဗ္ဗတံ။
၉. အနိက္ကသာဝေါ ကာသာဝံ၊ ယော ဝတ္ထံ ပရိဒဟိဿတိ။
အပေတော ဒမသစ္စေန၊ န သော ကာသာဝမရဟတိ။
၁၀. ယော စ ဝန္တကသာဝဿ၊ သီလေသု သုသမာဟိတော။
ဥပေတော ဒမသစ္စေန၊ သ ဝေ ကာသာဝမရဟတိ။

The first page of the Dhammapada in Pali, in Burmese script. Pali was a spoken language in India from about 400 B.C.E. to approximately 1000 C.E. The Dhammapada was originally transmitted orally. When it was eventually transcribed, it was written in a variety of scripts. Burmese is one of the Southeast Asian scripts in which the Pali scriptures have been preserved for many centuries.

Contents

Foreword by Andrew Harvey ix
Acknowledgments and Dedication xvii
About the Dhammapada xix

1. The Twin Verses 3
2. Vigilance 9
3. The Mind 13
4. Flowers 17
5. The Fool 21
6. The Wise One 27
7. The Enlightened One 31
8. Better than a Thousand 35
9. Evil 39
10. Punishment 43
11. Old Age 47
12. Self 51
13. The World 55
14. The Buddha 59
15. Happiness 63
16. Pleasure 67
17. Anger 71
18. Impurity 75

19. The Just 81
20. The Way 85
21. Miscellany 91
22. The Downward Course 95
23. The Elephant 99
24. Thirst 103
25. The Monk 111
26. The Brahman 117

Sources and Suggested Readings 126
List of Special Terms 128
About SkyLight Paths 130

Foreword

Andrew Harvey

In the *Anguttara Nikaya,* one of the oldest of the Pali Buddhist scriptures (and part of what is known as "The Third Basket of Discourses," the *Sutta Pitaka*), there is a haunting portrait of the Buddha. One day, a Hindu priest found the Buddha sitting under a tree in a state of deep peace: "His faculties were at rest, his mind was still and everything around him breathed self-discipline and serenity." The Buddha reminded the priest of an old male elephant; there was the same sense of great power being controlled and channeled into a force of gentleness.

The Brahman was amazed and asked the Buddha, "Are you a god?" "No," the Buddha answered. "Are you becoming an angel...or a spirit?" Once again, the Buddha replied that he was not; everything that limited him to a human existence of suffering had been, he said, "cut off at the root, chopped off like a palm stump done away with." The Buddha compared himself to a red lotus that had begun its life underwater but now rose above the water's surface. "So I too was born and grew up in the world, but I have transcended the world and I am no longer touched by it."

He had attained nirvana. Through dying to his false self and devoting his entire life to the unstinting service of others, the Buddha had freed himself to live in the vivid serenity and spaciousness of a consciousness beyond struggle and suffering. The priest plucked up his courage once more and asked the Buddha how, then, he should be categorized. "Remember me," the Buddha said quietly, "as someone who has woken up."

The confidence, clarity, and calm splendor of the Buddha's presence, as described in the *Anguttara Nikaya,* permeate the Dhammapada. Although monks compiled and edited this text about a hundred years after the Buddha's death and may have doctored it for polemical purposes, anyone reading the Dhammapada seriously and consistently has an overwhelming sense of the spiritual personality behind its teachings—a personality at once austere, forthright, and profoundly compassionate. The Buddha was both deeply troubled by the suffering, anguish, and evil in the world and also certain of the path that leads to overcoming and transcending them. In the section "Old Age," the Buddha appears to be directly and personally describing his own spiritual realization—the same realization the Hindu priest felt so richly, and from whose luminous silence and authority all of the words of the Dhammapada's teachings flow, and in whose shining they are all bathed:

> Looking for the maker of this house, I ran to no avail through a string of many births, and wearisome is birth again and again. But now, maker of the house, you have been seen. You shall not raise this house again. All the rafters are broken; the ridgepole is shattered. The mind, approaching eternity, has attained the extinction of all desires.

My own relationship with the message and truths of the Dhammapada has had three distinct stages, which I suspect mirror the progressive understanding of many modern seekers grappling with this seminal and always challenging text.

In the first stage, my admiration for the Buddha and his teachings was uncritical. I was in awe of the Buddha's immense spiritual prestige and profoundly moved by his pragmatic radicalism, his desire to teach the highest truths to everyone in a popular language, his refusal of all superstition, pseudo-mystical "explanations," and cultic rituals, and his relentlessly honest insistence on a rigorous, disciplined, self-responsible path to awakening. At the time I first studied the Dhammapada in depth, I was making a pilgrimage to the Buddhist sites in northern India. Three statements from the Dhammapada became the focus and inspiration of my journey:

> All that we are is the result of what we have thought.

> Through meditation, wisdom is won. Through lack of meditation, wisdom is lost.
>
> Your own self is your master. Who else could it be? With self well subdued, you gain a master hard to find.

The no-nonsense force of these statements—as well as their wisdom—delighted me. Reading from the Dhammapada in the Indian cities of Bodh Gaya and Sarnath, and in buses and trains along the way, I was struck again and again by the earthiness of the way in which the Buddha taught the highest truths. Like Jesus, Ramakrishna, and Muhammad, the Buddha had a genius for illustrating the most elevated concepts with the simplest imaginable images and metaphors:

> The evil done by one's self, born of one's self, suckled by one's self, crushes the foolish including oneself, even as a diamond cuts a stone.
>
> If a fool is associated with a wise person for an entire lifetime, that fool will perceive the truth as little as a spoon perceives the taste of soup.

I had been brought up in the European tradition of irony and fierce psychological analysis; the Buddha's hardheaded transcendental realism, so graphic and naked in its transmission, spoke to me directly, in a way that some of the Hindu mystical texts, with their recondite language and baroque ecstasies, could not.

Fifteen years later, in light of both my own inner revolution in mystical consciousness and an intensive study of the Divine Feminine in all traditions, I found myself taking a more critical look at the Buddha's teachings. My inner experience of the Mother-aspect of God and of the sacredness of the immanent and created world—and my increasing distress at how the Sacred Feminine had been degraded or betrayed in all of the major mystical and religious transmissions systems—led me to read the Dhammapada in a different light.

I came to understand how rooted in his own autobiographical experience the Buddha's teachings were. They reflected and enshrined as law the circumstances of his own awakening, which took the form of a very "masculine" rejection of home, marriage, sexuality, and householder responsibility in favor of a heroic search beyond the confines of relationship or society.

I became conscious of what I called an "addiction to transcendence"—and a kind of unconscious dualism that resulted from it, even in mystical philosophies that seemed to celebrate the unity of reality—running through all of the spirituality of the first axial age (the age from the seventh to the third centuries B.C.E. when a new spirituality flowered in China, India, and Greece). How could any philosophy that rejected much of earth life and a great deal of the feminine authentically reflect divine unity?

In this second stage of my reading of the Dhammapada, I never lost my awe for the Buddha or my joy at what had first moved me in his teachings. What I became aware of, however, was a slant that showed itself in the body-hatred, fear of sex, fear of women, obsession with emotional detachment, and almost exclusive privileging of celibacy and solitude as the one way of life that could lead to illumination. The Buddhist scholars I spoke to at length about this either side-stepped the questions I raised ("They are not really important in the overall vision"), historicized them ("How could the Buddha not have been slightly patriarchal given his time?"), or dismissed the passages in which an antifeminist stance occurs as "polemical implants" of later monks anxious to claim the Buddha's authority for their own ascetic path.

Explaining away important issues surrounding the denial or denigration of the Sacred Feminine in the Dhammapada—and by implication in the whole range of the Buddha's teachings—does not serve either the interest of truth or the Buddha's own realization. Didn't the Awakened One enjoin us to take nothing on trust, even from him, and to test his statements in the crucible of our own experience? Didn't the Buddha say on several occasions that his teachings were to be used as a raft to get to the other shore, to be discarded or modified when the truth had been reached? To imply that the teachings of the Buddha, as set forth in the Dhammapada, have limitations is not to deny their grandeur or truth; rather, it is to expand them to embrace kinds of truth and approaches to creation that we now see clearly are essential to the survival of a human race.

We are living through, I believe, a second axial age in which the patriarchal distortions of the first have to be corrected and filled out in all the mystical and religious transmission systems. The keys to the effectiveness of the second axial age is the restoration of the full dignity and power of the Sacred Feminine, so that the "sacred marriage" of masculine and feminine, transcendence and immanence, clarity and passion, and wisdom and compassion can take place within every human being and engender a divinized humanity capable at last of co-creating with the Divine a transformed world.

A careful look at the Dhammapada, however, reveals just how persuasive the denial is of everything associated with the feminine and creation: "This body is a painted image, covered with wounds, bunched together, sickly, weak, and impermanent.... This heap of corruption falls to pieces, life ending in death." In the Buddha's description of creation, he stresses its illusory nature: "Look upon the world as you would on a bubble. Look upon it as a mirage." While it is true that all reality reveals itself as a play of Light to one whose consciousness has become aware of the Light, this does not mean that reality is a mirage. All it means is that the reality our untransformed senses have registered is illusory. "True" reality is not unreal but super-real, utterly saturated with divine presence, the epiphany of divine beauty and truth. The Buddha's beliefs about the emptiness of the real world and its illusoriness are partly dictated by a pessimism about matter and the world. It is this largely unexamined pessimism that underlies his description of life ("There is no pain like this bodily existence.... Bodily demands are the greatest of evils") and his understanding of enlightenment as a state of removal from and of the world ("Give up what is ahead, give up what is behind, give up what is between, when you go to the other shore of existence").

My reading of the Dhammapada now has entered the third stage, one that unites and fuses the admiration of my first encounter with the critical understanding I have explored here. Once I saw and accepted the patriarchal distortion in the Buddha's teachings and saw how they can color and limit the vision of women, desire, the body, and enlightenment itself, I am now free to celebrate what remains timeless and all-embracing in them.

There are, I have come to believe, three main ways in which the Dhammapada's teachings are timeless and relevant to all seekers on all paths:

The first way is in the Buddha's unwavering awareness of suffering and evil. Karen Armstrong writes in her wonderful biography of the Buddha:

> There is a creeping new orthodoxy in modern society that is sometimes called "positive thinking." At its worst, this habit of optimism allows us to bury our heads in the sand, deny the ubiquity of pain in ourselves and others, and to immure ourselves in a state of deliberate heartlessness to ensure our emotional survival. The Buddha would have had little time for this. In his view, the spiritual life cannot begin until people allow themselves to be invaded by the reality of suffering, realize how fully it permeates our whole experience, and feel the pain of all other beings, even those whom we do not find congenial.

The banal pseudo-cheerfulness of much of New Age spirituality cannot help us in a time like ours when we are going to have to, without illusion or false consolation, face up to everything we are doing to each other and to nature if we are to have a chance of survival.

The second area in which the teachings of the Dhammapada are timelessly relevant are in the Buddha's constant insistence on the necessity of training and "guarding" the mind. No other person in human history has analyzed with such calm ruthlessness how our ongoing reality mirrors the inner state of our thoughts and intentions. The unexamined life held no charm whatsoever for the Buddha. He knew how savage and destructive its thoughtlessness could be, and he knew how hard it is to keep the mind constantly in the stream of compassion and insight, and so he stressed the necessity for meditation and intense dedication to spiritual practice. This greatest of all pragmatists makes it clear to all seekers that on the path to self-realization no magical solutions or quick fixes will work. What will work in the end is work. As the Buddha said on his deathbed, refusing one last time to flatter or make any false promises, "Work out your own salvation with diligence." As it is said in the Dhammapada: "By one's self evil is left undone; by one's self one is purified.... Be not thoughtless, watch your thoughts! Draw yourself out of the evil way, like an elephant sunk in mud."

The third timeless aspect of the Dhammapada's teachings lies, I believe, in the Buddha's championship of compassion, not simply as the deepest and noblest of all enlightened virtues but as an active transforming force in the world. The core of his teachings can be found in the soaring words of the first section, "The Twin Verses":

> "She abused me, he beat me, she defeated me, he robbed me." In those who harbor such thoughts, hatred will never cease. "She abused me, he beat me, she defeated me, he robbed me." In those who do not harbor such thoughts, hatred will cease. For never does hatred cease by hatred at any time. Hatred ceases by love. This is an eternal law.

This is perhaps the essential teaching of all the great mystic liberators of humanity—of the Buddha as well as of Jesus and Muhammad. As our world plunges into greater and greater violence and risks the total annihilation of human life and nature, the necessity to know the unifying wisdom of love and to live its force in every thought, gesture, vote, and spiritual, political, and economic action becomes ever more absolute.

In the Dhammapada, the Buddha tells us, "Enlightened ones are solid like the earth that endures, steadfast like a well-set column of stone, clear as a lake where all the mud has settled." Without such solidity, endurance, steadfastness, and clarity—fed by springs of transcendent insight and immanent compassion and sustained by spiritual discipline—we are all at the mercy of the hurricane of history, victims of karma and not loving masters of it in and under the Divine.

In one of the most poignant stories in the Pali Canon, a king in a state of terrible depression drove one day through a park full of tall tropical trees. The king got out of his carriage and walked among the roots, many of which were as tall as he was. "They were quiet; no discordant voices disturbed their peace." Looking at these magnificent ancient trees, the king was reminded at once of the grandeur and peacefulness of the Buddha. At once, he went back to his chariot and drove immediately to where the Buddha was staying.

In the torment and confusion of our time, the "tall trees and spacious roots" of the Buddha's teachings in the Dhammapada still radiate their empowering peace. To all those who come to them with an open mind and heart, they offer not only what Karen Armstrong calls "a haven of peace in a violent world of clamorous egotism" but also enduring images and proofs of serenity, dignity, and wisdom that can withstand and transcend anything.

> We live happily indeed when we are not hating those who hate us! Among those who hate us let us dwell free from hatred!... We live happily indeed when we are free from greed among the greedy! Among those who are greedy let us dwell free from greed! We live happily indeed when we call nothing our own! We shall be like the bright gods, feeding on happiness! [Dhammapada, chapter 15, verses 1–4 (197–200)]

Acknowledgments and Dedication

My work on this book was greatly assisted by the excellent editorial input of Polly Short Mahoney, Emily Wichland, and Dave O'Neal of SkyLight Paths. I'm also grateful to Michael Ponn for helping me with Pali-to-English translations and to Rosalind Jiko McIntosh for giving me extended access to several editions of the Dhammapada housed in the library of Zen Mountain Monastery in Mt. Tremper, New York. Tom Cowan was a bodhisattva of support as I worked on this text. And, as always, I give thanks to my teacher, John Daido Loori, Roshi, for guiding me to appreciate the beauties of the dharma that are so well illuminated in the Dhammapada.

I dedicate my work on this book to my friend Michael Yukon Grody.

> "Monks who, even when young, apply themselves to the doctrines of the Buddha brighten up this world, like the moon when free from the clouds." [Dhammapada, chapter 25, verse 23 (382)]

—Jack Maguire

The Buddha (Painting by Narayan Chitrakar)

About the Dhammapada

One of the most beloved and accessible texts in Buddhism, the Dhammapada was first put into writing during the period from approximately 50 B.C.E. to 50 C.E., when the earliest recorded body of Buddhist scriptures, the Pali Canon, was created. Pali, closely related to Sanskrit, is the liturgical language of Theravada, the oldest of Buddhism's three major divisions, commonly called vehicles. Today, Theravada prevails in Sri Lanka, Myanmar, Thailand, and other portions of Southeast Asia.

Because of our historically closer relationships with China, Japan, Vietnam, and Tibet, we in the United States and Canada are more familiar with the other two vehicles, Mahayana (the primary vehicle in the first three Asian nations) and Vajrayana, also known as Tibetan Buddhism. Both of these vehicles use Sanskrit as a liturgical language, so we are more accustomed to Sanskrit words in Buddhist literature than their Pali equivalents. Certain Sanskrit words like dharma, karma, and nirvana have even been adopted into the English language. Because of this situation, some common or significant Sanskrit words appear throughout this book, but their Pali equivalents are often provided first to reflect the language of the source.

The Dhammapada occasionally alludes to concepts or practices that belong distinctly to Theravada, but the text as a whole is revered in all three vehicles. A comparatively small work of only 422 verses, the Dhammapada forms part of the *Khuddaka Nikaya* ("Short Collection") in the Pali Canon's *Sutta Pitaka* ("Basket of Writings"). Among the Pali Canon's three basic divisions, the *Sutta Pitaka* is believed to contain the actual discourses of the historical Buddha.

The Pali word *dhamma* (Skt. *dharma*) means "law" in the sense of universal truth, and it is also used in a specific sense to refer to the Buddha's teachings, which Buddhists believe reflect this law. *Pada,* both a Pali and a Sanskrit term, literally means "footstep" or "track" as well as "word" or "verse." Thus the title *Dhammapada* might be translated generally as "Way of the Law" or more precisely as "Path of the Buddha's Teachings."

The word *buddha,* another term common to Pali and Sanskrit, means "the awakened one." It was—and is—a title bestowed upon the great religious teacher Siddhatta Gotama (whose name is more commonly seen in its Sanskrit form, Siddhartha Gautama), founder of the religion that now claims an estimated four hundred million adherents around the world.

Born in 566 B.C.E. into the ruling clan of a city-state in what we now call southern Nepal, the young Siddhartha forsook his wealth, privilege, and family to live as an itinerant monk, seeking an explanation for humanity's suffering as well as a way to end it. During a long night of intense meditation, he became enlightened and realized what came to be known as the Four Noble Truths: There is suffering in the world; suffering has a cause; suffering has an end; and a path exists to end suffering. He went on to teach throughout northeastern India for the next forty-five years, gaining many disciples and widespread respect before his death at the age of eighty in 486 B.C.E. Among other things, he taught that all human beings are capable of evolving into buddhas or, in other words, of "waking up" to full consciousness of their oneness with other beings and the universe. This realization involves a dropping away of the illusion of "self" as a separate entity. Because we are interconnected with everyone and everything else, it is all the more important to be wise and compassionate in every thought, word, and deed.

What the Dhammapada Is About

The Dhammapada doesn't encapsulate the Buddha's teachings in any comprehensive or essential manner. In fact, no single written work in Buddhism does. Buddhism is not a "religion of the book," like Judaism, Christianity, or Islam, all of which are based on a primary body of scriptures. Instead, Buddhism is a religion of individual practice and enlightenment, aided by direction from a living teacher and, to a lesser degree, personal study of Buddhist texts, which point to the truth without transcribing it directly. The virtue of the Dhammapada is that it beautifully, concisely, and viscerally gives the reader a sense of the route a person travels as he or she advances toward realization of his or her inherent perfection.

Far from being a random assemblage of statements and images, the Dhammapada is a carefully constructed work imbued with both spiritual and literary values. Each new topic unfolds in its proper sequence and rhythm, according to what the reader has already absorbed and what remains to be presented. The text begins by describing the fundamental role of mental conditioning in making us who we are. It then paints contrasting portraits of three types or levels of existence: the fool, the wise one, and the enlightened one. It goes on to address specific aspects of experience, conduct, and belief that characterize an individual's transformation from one of these modes of being to another.

The strikingly unified composition and impassioned moral tone of the Dhammapada strongly suggest that it is indeed the product of a single, highly skilled author. Given the power, vigor, and integrity of the oral tradition in Buddhism for centuries after the Buddha's death, it is not difficult to accept the proposal that the Dhammapada consists mostly if not entirely of his actual words. Many of its linguistic devices—for example, repetition, parallelism, alliteration, and well-crafted shifts in meter—lend themselves to easy memorization and faithful oral transmission.

About the Translation

The translation used here is based on one published by the eminent scholar Max Müller in 1870, which captures well the poetic flavor of the original. Some revisions have been made here based on my study of the Pali text and other translations or adaptations of particular distinction, including those of Irving Babbitt (1936), Juan Mascaró (1973), Eknath Easwaran (1985), Thomas Byrom (1993), and Thomas Cleary (1994). For more on these sources and other recommended readings, see "Sources and Suggested Readings" (p. 126).

About the Verses and Notes

Where appropriate, specific revisions, alternatives, clarifications, or facts of interest are mentioned in the notes that accompany individual verses. In each double-page spread, numbered notes are on the left page; verses of text (with numerical references to notes), on the right. Throughout the text, changes have been made in favor of gender neutrality, even though the Dhammapada was originally addressed primarily to monks. Also, for the sake of convenient reference to other sources, each verse is numbered first according to its order in the chapter and second (in parentheses) according to its order in the work as a whole. Occasionally a quotation or illustration is used to help relate the text to Buddhism in general.

The Dhammapada doesn't cover many pages, but it invites the mind and heart to savor it over a long period, even an entire lifetime. In this respect it is at once a perpetually revealing map and an eternally resonant message. As Easwaran notes in the introduction to his translation:

> These verses can be read and appreciated simply as wise philosophy; as such, they are part of the great literature of the world. But for those who would follow it to the end, the Dhammapada is a sure guide to nothing less than the highest goal life can offer: self-realization.

Dhammapada

1 The title "Twin Verses" refers to the structure of the chapter, which consists of ten pairs of statements. Each pair phrases the same basic truth, first from a negative point of view, then from a positive one, to illustrate the alternatives each individual faces. This incantatory rhetorical device is common in ancient Indian philosophy.

2 This belief supports Buddhism's emphasis on mental training, including the disciplines of right understanding, right thought, right mindfulness, and right meditation, four parts of the Noble Eightfold Path revealed to the Buddha during his enlightenment experience. (See ch. 14, n. 8 for a full description of the Noble Eightfold Path.)

3 The Pali word *dhamma* (Skt. *dharma*), here "eternal law," is also translated as "the truth" or "the way" in a universal sense; or it may refer to the eternal teaching transmitted by the Buddha (in this case, the word is usually capitalized).

4 Mara ("destroyer, death-causer") is an evil tempter, a supernatural being carried over from Hindu to Buddhist cosmology. He appeared mentally to the Buddha during his enlightenment and tried to thwart it. Mara represents bondage to the phenomenal world of pleasure and pain. He is the "death-causer" because it is only due to this bondage that one experiences death. The opposite of the phenomenal cycle of birth, death, and rebirth is nirvana (see ch. 2, n. 1.).

1 □ The Twin Verses[1]

1 (1) All that we are is the result of what we have thought.[2] It is founded on our thoughts. It is made up of our thoughts. If one speaks or acts with an evil thought, pain follows one, as the wheel follows the foot of the ox that draws the wagon.

2 (2) All that we are is the result of what we have thought. It is founded on our thoughts. It is made up of our thoughts. If one speaks or acts with a pure thought, happiness follows one, like a shadow that never leaves.

3 (3) "She abused me, he beat me, she defeated me, he robbed me": In those who harbor such thoughts, hatred will never cease.

4 (4) "She abused me, he beat me, she defeated me, he robbed me": In those who do not harbor such thoughts, hatred will cease.

5 (5) For never does hatred cease by hatred at any time. Hatred ceases by love. This is an eternal law.[3]

6 (6) Everyone in the world does not know that we must all come to end here; but those who do know, their quarrels cease at once.

7 (7) One who lives looking for pleasures only—uncontrolled sensually, immoderate in diet, idle, and weak—this one Mara[4] will surely overthrow, as the wind blows down a feeble tree.

8 (8) One who does not live looking for pleasures only—well-controlled sensually, moderate in diet, diligent, and strong—this one Mara will surely not overthrow, any more than the wind blows down a mountain of stone.

5 A saffron (golden yellow) robe is worn by a Buddhist monk. This color is most commonly associated with monastics of the Theravada vehicle (see p. xix).

6 The next world refers to the next lifetime, when one may be reborn into one of the five "worlds" or realms of being: demons in various hells, hungry ghosts, animals, human beings, and gods in various heavens. Some schools of Buddhism speak of six realms, adding another realm of demons or demigods.

9 (9) One who wishes to don the saffron robe[5] while still impure, intemperate, and untruthful is unworthy to do so.

10 (10) One who has cleansed the mind and is endowed with temperance and truthfulness is indeed worthy to wear the saffron robe.

11 (11) One who imagines the real as false and sees falsehood as reality never arrives at truth but follows vain desires.

12 (12) One who knows reality as real and falsehood as false arrives at truth and follows worthy aspirations.

13 (13) As rain breaks through a poorly thatched house, lust breaks through an unvigilant mind.

14 (14) As rain does not break through a skillfully thatched house, lust does not break through a vigilant mind.

15 (15) Evildoers mourn in this world and mourn in the next one.[6] They mourn in both. They mourn and grieve when they see the filthiness of their own deeds.

16 (16) Virtuous ones delight in this world and delight in the next one. They delight in both. They delight and rejoice when they see the purity of their own deeds.

17 (17) Evildoers suffer in this world and in the next. They suffer in both. They suffer when they think of the evil they have done. They suffer even more when they continue on the evil path.

18 (18) Virtuous ones are happy in this world and in the next. They are happy when they think of the good they have done. They are even happier when they continue on the good path.

19 (19) Thoughtless ones, even if they can recite many sacred verses but do not follow them, have no claim to a religious life, but are like cowherders counting the cows of others.

7 The law: *dhamma.* See n. 3 above.

When receiving the teachings, it is important to have the correct attitude. It is not practicing the Dharma properly to listen with the intention of gaining material advantage or reputation. Neither should our goal be higher rebirth in the next life, nor should we be wishing only for our own liberation from *samsara.* These are all attitudes we should reject. Instead, let us listen to the teachings with the determined wish to attain the state of omniscience for the sake of all beings.

—His Holiness the Dalai Lama

20 (20) Thoughtful ones, even if they can recite only a few verses but do follow the law[7] and, forsaking lust, hatred, and delusion, possess true knowledge and peace of mind—they, clinging to nothing in this world or the next, have indeed a claim to a religious life.

In Tibetan Buddhism, Vajrapani, protector of the Dharma, represents the spiritual battle against the forces of lust, hatred, and delusion. (Painting by Madhu and Sangita Chitrakar)

1 "Freedom beyond life and death" is used here as a translation of the term *nibbana* (Skt. *nirvana*), literally "extinguished," as a flame when it is blown out. In Buddhism, it represents the state of endless peace and "emptiness" (i.e., no separate "things" to cling to) that one aspires to reach through enlightenment. Its opposite is the phenomenal cycle of birth, death, and rebirth (Pali and Skt., *samsara*) that is characterized by desire, impermanence, and suffering.

The mind is the nucleus of *samsara* and nirvana.

—Lama Thubten Yeshe

2 Noblest ones: *ariyas* (Skt. *aryas*) or "elect ones," those who are on the path toward enlightenment.

3 The law: *dhamma*. See ch. 1, n. 3.

4 The phrase "terraced heights" metaphorically evokes the multi-leveled agricultural fields that over three millennia have been carved into hillsides throughout northern India and adjacent areas of Asia. The mind should be cultivated in vigilance with similar care, so one can advance upward stage by stage.

2 □ Vigilance

1 (21) Vigilance is the path of freedom beyond life and death;[1] thoughtlessness, the path of death. Those who are vigilant do not die. Those who are thoughtless are as if dead already.

2 (22) Having understood this clearly, those who have progressed in vigilance are happy about it, rejoicing in the wisdom of the noblest ones.[2]

3 (23) These wise people—meditative, perseverant, always exerting power—attain freedom from life and death, the supreme happiness.

4 (24) When people are vigilant and exert themselves, and remain ever mindful, and always do pure deeds, and act with consideration and restraint, and live according to the law,[3] then their glory will increase.

5 (25) By rousing themselves, by vigilance, by temperance and self-control, wise people make for themselves an island that no flood can overwhelm.

6 (26) Foolish people follow after vanity. Wise people guard vigilance as their greatest treasure.

7 (27) Follow not after vanity, nor after the enjoyment of sensual pleasures and lust! The one who is vigilant and meditative knows ample joy.

8 (28) When people of right understanding drive away vanity by staying vigilant, they climb the terraced heights[4] of wisdom and look

5 Maghavan: an epithet for Indra, king of the gods in the Hindu pantheon. Buddhism is not a theistic system—that is, it does not teach belief in a creator god or gods—but it makes many references to the gods of Hinduism, the older, more established religion of the Buddha's time and place. Also, Buddhism says that one can be born into a godlike existence. If so, one lives a longer, more comfortable life than humans do, but one is not omnipotent or enlightened, nor in any way a creator, savior, or judge. See ch. 1, n. 6.

6 "Walkers of the way" is used here as a looser, more present-day friendly translation of *bhikkus* (Skt. *bhikshus*), Buddhist monks who, like the Buddha and his followers, pursue a homeless existence of wandering and begging. Müller translates the term as "mendicants."

down on the fools. Free from sorrows, they see below them the sorrowing crowd, as those who stand on mountains see below them the people on the plain.

9 (29) Vigilant among the slothful, awake among the sleeping, the wise one advances like a racer, leaving behind the mere trotter.

10 (30) By vigilance did Maghavan[5] rise to the lordship of the gods. People praise vigilance; thoughtlessness is always blamed.

11 (31) Walkers of the way[6] who delight in vigilance, fearing thoughtlessness, move like a fire, burning away all obstacles large and small.

12 (32) Walkers of the way who delight in vigilance, fearing thoughtlessness, cannot fall back—they are close to freedom already.

1 A fletcher is one who makes arrows. Some translations say "archer," indicating the person who actually shoots arrows (and, therefore, can be said to make arrows rest "straight" against the bow so they will fly "straight" to their target). The former translation better reflects the Buddha's teaching in this chapter that we must be the makers of our own minds.

2 Mara: see ch. 1, n. 4.

3 The expression "hidden away in the body" refers to the mind's tendency to identify itself in terms of the physical body, as if it were some elusive ghost lurking within. The Buddha bids us not to have such a narrow sense of self (or mind), but rather to realize that self is one with everything else in the universe. Here, the notion is to tame the mind out of its problematic tendency to act selfishly on its own—"hiding" or "traveling far."

4 The true law: *dhamma.* See ch. 1, n. 3.

5 The phrase "renounced the notions of merit and demerit" (or, as other translators say, "renounced good and evil") refers to the Buddha's teaching that one should not think in terms of dualistic opposites, which tend to be oversimplistic and separatist. Buddhism doesn't deny that one can *perceive* a certain situation as being either positive or negative, but one should recognize this as a perception, not a reality in itself. In addition, one should not be intent upon accruing merit for self-gain.

3 □ The Mind

1 (33) As fletchers[1] make straight their arrows, wise ones make straight their trembling, unsteady minds, which are difficult to guard, difficult to hold back.

2 (34) Like a fish taken from the water and thrown on the dry ground, our mind quivers all over in its effort to escape the dominion of Mara.[2]

3 (35) It is good to tame the mind, which is flighty and difficult to restrain, rushing wherever it will. A tamed mind brings happiness.

4 (36) Let wise ones monitor the mind, which is subtle, difficult to perceive, and restless. A mind well monitored brings happiness.

5 (37) Those who bridle their mind, which, being insubstantial, would travel far on its own, hidden away in the body,[3] are free from the bonds of Mara.

6 (38) If one's mind is unsteady, if one does not know the true law,[4] one's wisdom will never be perfect.

7 (39) If one's mind is free from lust and unperplexed, if one has renounced the notions of merit and demerit,[5] if one remains awake and watchful, then one never has to fear.

8 (40) Knowing that one's body is fragile like a clay pot, and making one's mind firm like a fortress, one should attack Mara with the weapon of wisdom. One should then never falter in watching the conquered Mara.

Meditation provides a way for us to train in the middle way—in staying right on the spot. We are encouraged not to judge whatever arises in our mind; in fact, we are encouraged not to even grasp whatever arises in our mind. What we usually call good or bad we simply acknowledge as thinking, without all the usual drama that goes along with right and wrong. We are instructed to let the thoughts come and go as if touching a bubble with a feather.

—Pema Chödrön

9 (41) Before long—alas!—the body will lie on the ground, bereft of consciousness and despised, like a useless rotten log.

10 (42) Whatever a hater may do to another hater, or an enemy to an enemy, one's own mind wrongly directed will do to one even greater harm.

11 (43) Neither a mother, nor a father, nor any other relative will do to one as great a service as one's own well-directed mind.

1 Thomas Cleary remarks: "The title of this chapter stands for things of the world, which we may heedlessly pursue as vanities even as time and death stalk us, or we may mindfully use constructively to beautify the world if we realize their value."

2 In Buddhist mythology, derived from Hindu mythology, Yama is the ruler of death and the various hellish realms. For an explanation of the five (or, in some schools, six) "realms of being" in Buddhism, see ch. 1, n. 6.

3 Path of the law: *dhammapada*.

4 The image of the garland as an "interweaving of things" is a popular one in Buddhism. One of the most beloved Mahayana scriptures is the *Flower Garland Sutra* or *Avatamsaka Sutra,* which teaches that the Buddha, mind, all sentient beings, and the universe are one and the same.

5 The phrase "earnest disciple" is translated by Juan Mascaró as "wise student," meaning "student" in the Buddhist sense: one who follows the Buddha as teacher.

6 Mara: see ch. 1, n. 4. For a comparable allusion to Mara, see ch. 20, verse 2 (and see n. 4).

7 The fifth-century Theravada commentator Buddhaghosha recorded a famous mythological story that he attributed to the Buddha, and upon which this verse is based. It's worth summarizing here as an example of many similar commentaries on Dhammapada verses:

> In one of the myriad Buddhist heavens there lived a god called Garland-weaver who had one thousand wives. One of these wives was on a high bough of a tree picking flowers to adorn her husband when she got distracted by the pleasure of the act. She fell to Earth, where she was born into a wealthy family. After

4 □ Flowers[1]

1 (44) Who shall overcome this world, and the world of Yama,[2] and the world of the gods? Who shall find the well-taught path of the law,[3] even as a clever garland weaver picks out the right flower?[4]

2 (45) The earnest disciple[5] shall overcome this world, the world of Yama, and the world of the gods. The earnest disciple shall find the well-taught path of the law, even as a clever garland weaver picks out the right flower.

3 (46) The one who knows that this body is like froth, as unsubstantial as a mirage, will break the flower-tipped arrow of Mara[6] and never see the king of death.

4 (47) Death carries off a person who is gathering flowers with a distracted mind, just as a flood carries off a sleeping village.

5 (48) Death overpowers a person who is gathering flowers for pleasure before this person can achieve any satisfaction.[7]

6 (49) As the bee collects nectar and flies away without harming the flower, its color, or its scent, so let a wise person go among the people and things of this life.

7 (50) Let not a wise person note the perversities of others, nor what they have done or left undone.

8 (51) Like a beautiful flower without scent are the fair but fruitless words of the one who speaks of virtue but does not act accordingly.

she married, people noticed that she constantly made offerings of garlands, saying, "May these alms bring about my rebirth with my husband." Wrongly assuming she meant her mortal husband, people gave her the name "Husband-honorer."

When Husband-honorer died at an advanced age, she was reborn into the presence of the god Garland-weaver. "We have not seen you since morning," he complained. Husband-honorer told him about her life as a mortal. Describing it as "a mere one hundred years long," she said, "Humans are always reckless, as if they were born to a life of an incalculable number of years, and were never to grow old and die."

To sum up the story, the Buddha recited this verse (see ch. 1, n. 6, and ch. 2, n. 5, for more on gods).

The lotus, a beautiful water lily that grows in the mud, is a symbol in Buddhism for the true, inner perfection of each human being, even though he or she lives in a world of corruption. (Painting by Kiran Chitrakar)

9 (52) Like a beautiful flower full of scent are the fair and fruitful words of the one who speaks of virtue and acts accordingly.

10 (53) Even as one may fashion many fine wreaths from a heap of flowers, so should one born to the mortal lot make from it many fine deeds.

11 (54) The scent of flowers does not travel against the wind, nor that of sandalwood, rosebay, or jasmine. But the fragrance of good people travels even against the wind. Thus a good person pervades the universe.

12 (55) Among the scents of sandalwood, rosebay, the blue lotus, and jasmine, the perfume of virtue is the best.

13 (56) Not far from this world travels the scent of rosebay or sandalwood. But the perfume of virtue rises up to the highest gods.

14 (57) The path of those who are virtuous, diligent, and liberated by the true law can never be found by Mara.

15/16 (58/59) Even as a lotus may grow from roadside garbage and spread joy to many traveling souls with its scent, so a true follower of the Buddha shines and brings light to multitudes of blind mortals.

1 The fool: *bala,* which can also mean "child." For this reason, some translators, including Easwaran, translate it in this context as "the immature."

2 The true law: *dhamma*. See ch. 1, n. 3.

3 This statement conveys the Buddhist belief that there is no separate entity known as the individual "self." Instead, we are all interdependent on everyone and everything else in the universe.

5 □ The Fool[1]

1 (60) Long is the night to the one who is awake. Long is the road to the one who is tired. Long is life to the foolish who do not know the true law.[2]

2 (61) If a traveler does not meet with someone better or equal in wisdom, that traveler should keep to a solitary journey. There is no true companionship with a fool.

3 (62) "These children belong to me!" and "This wealth belongs to me!" With such thoughts fools are tormented. They do not even belong to themselves.[3] How much less do children and wealth belong to them?

4 (63) Fools who know their foolishness are wise at least so far. But fools who think themselves wise—they are called fools indeed.

5 (64) If a fool is associated with a wise person for an entire lifetime, that fool will perceive the truth as little as a spoon perceives the taste of soup.

6 (65) If an intelligent person is associated with a wise one for only a minute, that intelligent person will soon perceive the truth just as the tongue perceives the taste of soup.

7 (66) Fools with little understanding are their own greatest enemies, for they do evil deeds which must bear bitter fruits.

8 (67) A deed is not well done if one must repent it, and if the reward is crying and a tearful face.

4 Eat food like an ascetic: the original text reads "eat food with the tip of a blade of kusha grass," referring to the traditional practice of ascetics, which guaranteed them a very small meal.

The Buddha himself did not advocate fasting as a spiritual discipline, preferring instead a "middle way" approach that avoided asceticism at one extreme and sensual indulgence at the other. Nevertheless, the Indian and Eastern Asian cultures of his time and afterward continued to associate asceticism with spiritual worthiness.

5 This verse and the following one allude to the doctrine of *kamma*, better known in the West in its Sanskrit form, *karma*. The closest Western equivalent is the law of cause and effect. See ch. 9, n. 1.

Essentially, karma is neutral: it is inaccurate to speak of "good karma" or "bad karma" as Westerners often do. Individual acts or outcomes can be judged as "good" or "bad," but the core doctrine is more simply that each cause has a corresponding effect that leads to another, corresponding cause, and so on.

Buddhists believe that wise thought, speech, and behavior naturally have a positive influence on the way karma operates in our life and, according to most Buddhist schools, on the quality of our next lifetime. Foolish thinking, speaking, and behaving have the opposite impact.

6 Monks: the original text reads "among those who have left the world." Superficially, this designation can be taken to mean those who live within a monastic community that sets itself apart from society as a whole. In fact, most Buddhist monks, from the Buddha's time up to the present, have circulated rather freely in society as mendicants, teachers, caregivers, and the like. It is perhaps more accurate to say that this designation refers to those who have ceased to live a life of worldly desires.

7 Laypeople: the original reads "householders," a common designation in Buddhism for nonmonastic believers. By way of contrast, monks are often referred to as "homeless."

8 Nirvana: the more familiar Sanskrit term for Pali *nibbana*. The contrast here is between the abundant worldly goods associated with wealth and the free, eternal "emptiness" associated with nirvana. See ch. 2, n. 1.

9 (68) No, a deed is well done if one does not repent it, and if the reward is happiness and good cheer.

10 (69) As long as their evil deeds do not bear fruit, fools think the deeds are like honey; but when they ripen, then these same fools suffer grief.

11 (70) Let fools month after month eat food like an ascetic,[4] still they are not worth the sixteenth part of those who have well weighed the law.

12 (71) An evil deed does not begin to sour right away like newly drawn milk. Instead, smoldering like fire covered with ashes, it follows the fool.[5]

13 (72) Far from profiting them, the knowledge that fools acquire destroys their good fortune and even their minds.

14 (73) Fools will desire a false reputation, precedence among monks,[6] lordship in the monasteries, and honor among laypeople.[7]

15 (74) Fools often say to themselves, "May both laypeople and monks think this-and-that worthy thing is done by me! May they be subject to me in everything that is to be done or is not to be done!" Thus is the mind of a fool, who builds more and more desire and pride.

16 (75) One road leads to wealth, the other leads to nirvana.[8] If disciples of the Buddha have learned this fact, they will not delight in the praise of people. They will strive for freedom from worldly matters.

❖ In Buddhism, the essential meaning of the word "study" is the unceasing, dedicated observation and investigation of whatever arises in the mind, be it pleasant or unpleasant. Only those familiar with the observation of mind can really understand Dharma.

—Buddhadasa Bhikkhu

Manjushri, the bodhisattva of wisdom, holds a flaming sword that cuts through misconception and destroys the darkness of ignorance, which binds us to worldly attachments. In his left hand he holds *The Perfection of Wisdom Sutra* (on top of the lotus), which is treasured among Vajrayana Buddhists as the Buddha's most profound statement on the ultimate nature of reality. (Painting by Madhu and Sangita Chitrakar)

✤ Wisdom does not mean knowledge but experiential understanding. Wisdom helps you to change radically your habits and perceptions, as you discover the constantly changing, interconnected nature of the whole of existence.

—Martine Batchelor

1 The law: *dhamma*. See ch. 1, n. 3.

2 Noble ones: *ariyas*, those who are on the path toward enlightenment.

3 The statement "wise people shape themselves" expresses the important Buddhist belief that we are responsible for creating ourselves. We can—and should—follow the advice and example of our teachers, but we can't assign to them the task of shaping who we are. Only we can do that for ourselves.

6 □ The Wise One

1 (76) If you encounter someone who is intelligent, shows you what is to be avoided, and gives reproof where it is due, follow that wise person as you would someone who reveals hidden treasures. It will be better, not worse, for you.

2 (77) Let this wise one admonish, teach, and forbid what is improper. Such a person will be loved by the good and hated by the bad.

3 (78) Do not have evildoers or low people for friends. Have virtuous people for friends. Have for friends the best of people.

4 (79) The person who drinks in the law[1] lives happily with a serene mind. Wise ones ever rejoice in the law as taught by the noble ones.[2]

5 (80) Irrigators guide the water; fletchers straighten the arrows; carpenters carve the wood; wise people shape themselves.[3]

6 (81) As a solid rock is not moved by the wind, wise people are not shaken by blame or by praise.

7 (82) Wise ones, after they have listened to the law, become serene, like a deep, clear, still lake.

8 (83) Wise people walk on, whatever may happen. They do not speak out of a desire for sensual gratification. Whether touched by happiness or sorrow, they never appear elated or depressed.

9 (84) Whether for the sake of self or for the sake of others, if a person wishes not for a child, wealth, power, or success by unfair means, then that person is good, wise, and upright.

4 The "other shore" refers to nirvana (Pali *nibbana*), the pure state beyond the world of life and death ("this shore") that is realized through enlightenment.

5 The dominion of death: *samsara,* the world of impermanent phenomena, to which we are bound in a recurring cycle of life and death that can only be broken through becoming enlightened.

6 The life of the law: the original reads *bhikku,* "wandering monk." The freer translation is used to make the text more relevant to contemporary Western readers. In the Buddha's time, only "wandering monks" were considered "followers of the law" and the Dhammapada was specifically addressed to them. See also ch. 2, n. 6.

7 In Buddhist tradition, the seven elements of knowledge (also called the seven fields of enlightenment) are: mindfulness, vigor, joy, serenity, concentration, equanimity, and absorption of the law.

10 (85) Few among all people reach the other shore.[4] The others merely run up and down this shore.

11 (86) But those who follow the law, when it has been well taught, will reach the other shore, and pass over the dominion of death,[5] however difficult it may be to cross.

12/13 (87/88) Wise ones should leave the dark state of ordinary life and follow the bright state of the life of the law.[6] After going from their homes to the homeless state, they should find joy in their renunciation where others would say joy was hard to find. Leaving all worldly pleasures behind, and calling nothing their own, wise ones should purge themselves of all the vices of the mind.

14 (89) Those whose minds are well grounded in the seven elements of knowledge,[7] who without clinging to anything rejoice in freedom from attachment, whose appetites have been conquered, and who are full of light—they enter nirvana even in this world.

1 The enlightened one: *arahant* (Skt. *arhat*). In Theravada, the *arahant* is the ideal figure—one who has become enlightened and, therefore, enters nirvana at death and is not reborn into *samsara,* the endless cycle of birth, death, and suffering. In Mahayana and Vajrayana, the other two vehicles of Buddhism, the ideal is the *bodhisattva,* one who has become enlightened but who puts off final entry into nirvana until all beings are saved and, therefore, continues to be reborn into *samsara* to assist others along the path.

2 The infinite void: *sunnata* (Skt. *shunyata*). The term refers to a core Buddhist doctrine—that all things are essentially empty or impermanent, with no "fixed abode," as suggested by the lifestyle of the wandering monk.

3 Complete freedom: *nibbana* (Skt. *nirvana*). See ch. 2, n. 1.

4 The phrase "moderate in what they consume" refers to the Buddhist concept of the "middle way," that is, avoiding the desire-oriented extremes of asceticism on one end and overindulgence on the other.

5 The gods are not "the greatest ones" in Buddhist cosmology. Although the gods may have longer, more comfortable, and more powerful lives than humans, the "greatest ones" are those who are enlightened (see verse 8). Some Buddhist texts say that humans alone have the capacity to become enlightened because they occupy a cosmic "middle ground," low enough to experience suffering and high enough to be motivated to overcome it. (For more on gods, see ch. 1, n. 6 and ch. 2, n. 5.)

6 The world of life, death, and impermanence: *samsara.* See n. 1 above.

7 The truth: *dhamma*. See ch. 1, n. 3.

7 □ The Enlightened One[1]

1 (90) There is no suffering for those who have finished their journey, foresworn grievous desires, and freed themselves fully from all bonds.

2 (91) The mindful ones ever exert themselves. They do not delight in having a fixed abode. Like swans who fly from their lake, they leave their house and home.

3 (92) Like the path of swans in the sky, the path of those who have no possessions, who feed on offerings, who perceive the infinite void,[2] and who live in complete freedom[3] is difficult to understand.

4 (93) Like the path of swans in the sky, the path of those who have mastered their cravings, who are moderate in what they consume,[4] who perceive the infinite void, and who live in complete freedom, is difficult to understand.

5 (94) The gods[5] envy these enlightened ones, who have trained their senses as good drivers have tamed their horses, and who are free from lust, greed, and pride.

6 (95) Enlightened ones are solid like the earth that endures, steadfast like a well-set column of stone, clear as a lake where all the mud has settled. They are liberated from the world of life, death, and impermanence.[6]

7 (96) As a result of the freedom they have attained through knowledge of the truth,[7] their thoughts are peaceful, their words are peaceful, and their deeds are peaceful.

8 Two types of humans are being contrasted here: those whose lives are dualistically divided between subject (self) and object (desired things), and those who are at one with the universe. The former only "look" and (possibly) "find" but never really "have" or "know," as the latter do.

The perfect enlightenment of buddhahood—selfless freedom—transcends all dichotomies and is just as powerful in the social realm as it is peaceful in personal experience. Its core insight is the full embrace of the inexorable relatedness of the selfless individual to all others.

—Robert A. F. Thurman

8 (97) Those who are free from illusion, who have seen the infinite void, who have ceased to cling to impermanent things, who have removed temptations, and who have renounced desires—they are indeed the greatest ones of all.

9 (98) Wherever enlightened ones dwell—in a village or wilderness, on a mountain or on a coast—that is indeed a place of joy.

10 (99) In forests where others find no delight, there they will know delight. Because they do not look for pleasure, they will have it.[8]

1 Throughout this chapter, the main point is that quality is better than quantity. In Sanskrit and other Indian languages, it's common to state specific, representationally appropriate numbers instead of using the more general terms "few," "many," or even "innumerable." For example, Buddhist texts frequently refer to all phenomena in the universe as "the ten thousand things." Thus, "a thousand" here represents "a huge amount."

2 The law: *dhamma.* See ch. 1, n. 3.

3 In Buddhism as well as Hinduism, Mara is the archetypal image (or god) of evil, while Brahma, the creator in Hindu mythology, can be considered the archetypal image (or god) of good.

4 Sacrificial fires, where ritual offerings are rendered, are a central aspect of Hindu worship and must be tended to properly.

8 ☐ Better than a Thousand[1]

1 (100) Even though a speech is composed of a thousand words, but those words are senseless, one word of sense is better; when people hear it, they become quiet.

2 (101) Even though a poem is composed of a thousand words, but those words are senseless, one word of sense is better; when people hear it, they become quiet.

3 (102) Even though someone recites a hundred poems made up of senseless words, one word of the law[2] is better; when people hear it, they become quiet.

4 (103) If someone conquers a thousand times a thousand others in battle, and someone else conquers his or her own self, the latter one is the greatest of all conquerors.

5/6 (104/105) One's self conquered is better than all other people conquered. Not even Mara, Brahma, or any other god[3] can change into defeat the victory of someone who has conquered his or her self.

7 (106) If someone for a hundred years sacrifices month after month at the cost of a thousand dollars a month, and if that same someone for one brief moment pays homage to a person who knows the law, better is that one act of homage than all the sacrifices.

8 (107) If someone for a hundred years tends the sacrificial fire[4] in the forest, and if that same someone for one brief moment pays homage to a person who knows the truth, better is that one act of homage than all the tending.

5 Sacrifices in this world: that is, sacrifices of worldly things.

6 The phrase "to gain merit" refers to advancing one's karma in a positive direction through performing noble deeds, so that one is more likely to be reborn into a more favorable life or to achieve enlightenment sooner. The implication here is that such a thing is possible and even commendable, but it's far more effective and efficient to cultivate one's inner self, so that one can realize genuine reverence for wisdom.

7 A quarter part: a fraction (see n. 1 above). The choice of the "quarter" or "one-fourth" amount is probably intended to provide a rhetorically fitting counterpoint to the "four things" that increase in verse 10.

8 This verse reflects the essential practicality of Buddhism. The characteristics that increase—health, beauty, happiness, and vigor—are all natural components of well-being, as opposed to the more abstract, artificial concerns involved in power, wealth, prestige, and merit, which are mentioned negatively in previous verses.

9 (108) Whatever one sacrifices in this world[5] continuously for an entire year in order to gain merit[6]—all of this sacrifice is not worth a quarter part[7] of reverence paid to the wise.

10 (109) If one maintains the practice of reverence and respect for the wise, four things will increase for that person: health, beauty, happiness, and vigor.[8]

11 (110) But as for a life of a hundred years lived viciously and unrestrained—a life of one day of virtue and self-control is better.

12 (111) And as for a life of a hundred years lived foolishly and wantonly—a life of one day of wisdom and rightness is better.

13 (112) And as for a life of a hundred years lived idly and weakly—a life of one day of diligence and strength is better.

14 (113) And as for a life of a hundred years lived without seeing the impermanence of all things—a life of one day seeing the impermanence of all things is better.

15 (114) And as for a life of a hundred years lived without seeing eternity—a life of one day seeing eternity is better.

16 (115) And as for a life of a hundred years lived without seeing the law—a life of one day seeing the law is better.

1 This chapter deals with the Buddhist concept of *kamma* (Skt. *karma*), which teaches that every action contributes to a chain of cause and effect (see ch. 5, n. 5). In this verse and the next one, attention focuses on the subconcept of *sankhara* (Skt. *samskara*), or karma-created patterns. When one engages in the same kind of thought, speech, or deed again and again, it generates *sankhara,* so that one is predisposed to repeat the pattern, with the inclination becoming more strongly entrenched each time.

2 The "ripening" of evil deeds (and, in verse 5, good deeds) refers to the karma they set in motion, which, if left unchecked, eventually leads to effects of a like nature that cannot be missed or avoided.

9 □ Evil

1 (116) Let one be vigorous in doing good. Let one take pains not to do evil. If one does what is good slothfully, one's mind can easily and eagerly turn toward evil thoughts.

2 (117) If one does commits a sin, let one not commit the same sin again. Let one not take delight in evil: The accumulation of evil is painful.[1]

3 (118) If one does what is good, let one do the same thing again. Let one take delight in good. The accumulation of good is joyful.

4 (119) Even evildoers see happiness as long as their evil deeds have not ripened;[2] but when their evil deeds have ripened, then do the evildoers see sorrow.

5 (120) Even doers of good see sorrow as long as their good deeds have not ripened; but when their good deeds have ripened, then do the doers of good see happiness.

6 (121) Let no one think lightly of evil, saying inwardly, "This will not bring me sorrow." Even by the falling of tiny water drops, a water pot is filled. Fools become full of evil, even if they gather it little by little.

7 (122) Let no one think lightly of good, saying inwardly, "This will not bring me happiness." Even by the falling of tiny water drops, a water pot is filled. Wise ones become full of good, even if they gather it little by little.

3 The notion here is that the poison must have a significantly open point of entry into the body—a wound rather than a pore—in order to cause harm. The "poison" in this verse symbolizes evil coming from the outside, while the "wound" symbolizes the karmic result one suffers for having done evil oneself.

4 According to Theravada Buddhism, the only people not reborn into one realm or another are those who attain nirvana. Mahayana and Vajrayana Buddhism teach that one who attains enlightenment can choose to delay final entry into nirvana in order to be reborn again and again to help save others. For more on the various realms of birth and death, see also ch. 1, n. 6; for more on the different concepts of rebirth among the Buddhist vehicles, see ch. 7, n. 1.

8 (123) Let one avoid evil deeds, as merchants, if they have few companions and carry much wealth, avoid dangerous roads, as people who love life avoid poison.

9 (124) One who has no wound on the hand may touch poison with the hand.[3] Poison does not affect one who has no wound, nor does evil befall one who does not commit evil.

10 (125) If one offends a harmless, pure, and innocent person, the evil falls back on that fool, like dust tossed against the wind falls back on the thrower.

11 (126) Some people are reborn.[4] Evildoers go to sorrowful existences. Doers of good go to happy ones. Those who are free from all worldly desires attain nirvana.

12 (127) Not in the sky, not in the sea, not in the clefts of the mountain is there known a spot in the whole world where one might live free from an evil deed.

13 (128) Not in the sky, not in the sea, not in the clefts of the mountain is there known a spot in the whole world where one might live free from being overcome by death.

1 After death: that is, in the next rebirth.

2 In Buddhism, those who become fully enlightened are eligible after death for final escape into nirvana, the state of undifferentiated or "empty" bliss. However, as this verse indicates, one can attain moments of nirvana during one's lifetime by rising above the world of passions and other impermanent states.

3 In Buddhist texts, fire is frequently used as a symbol for desires, passions, and impermanent states. One of the Buddha's most famous statements is "The entire world is on fire, the entire world is burning."

4 It is a common rhetorical device in Indian languages to offer specifically numbered lists, rather than simply to give unnumbered examples or partial lists followed by "and so on." Thus a numbered list like this one does not preclude the existence of other possible punishments.

10 □ Punishment

1 (129) All people tremble at the prospect of punishment. All people fear death. Remember that you are like them, and do not kill or cause slaughter.

2 (130) All people tremble at the prospect of punishment. All people fear death. Remember that you are like them, and do not strike or injure.

3 (131) Those who, seeking their own happiness, punish beings who also long for happiness, will not find happiness after death.[1]

4 (132) Those who, seeking their own happiness, do not punish beings who also long for happiness, will find happiness after death.

5 (133) Do not speak harshly to anyone. Those who are so addressed will answer in the same way. Angry speech breeds pain: Blows for blows will touch you.

6 (134) If, like a shattered gong, you say nothing harsh, then you have reached nirvana;[2] anger is not known to you.

7 (135) As cowherds with sticks drive their cows into the stable, so old age and death drive the lives of human beings.

8 (136) Fools do not know what awaits them when they commit evil deeds, but these stupid fools are consumed by their own deeds, as if burnt by fire.[3]

9 (137) Those who inflict punishment on people who do not deserve it and thereby offend against the innocent will soon experience one of these ten punishments:[4]

5 The phrase "misfortune dealt by the king" can be taken to mean legal or political trouble.

6 For more on the possible realms of rebirth, see ch. 1, n. 6.

7 These practices, sometimes called the "seven ascetic deeds," are ancient Hindu acts of self-mortification performed to overcome worldly desires. Although a few Buddhist schools continue to regard some of these austerities as effective and praiseworthy, most reject them as too extreme and, therefore, not in accord with the Buddhist concept of keeping to the "middle way" of temperance, modesty, and similar virtues.

8 Brahman (often Anglicized as "brahmin"): a member of the highest, priestly caste in Hindu society. The verse contrasts the titles "brahman," "ascetic," and "monk" with the real thing the titles represent: a person who practices the virtues listed here.

9 The law: *dhamma*. See ch. 1, n. 3.

10 (138) They will have cruel suffering, weakness, or injury of the body; or heavy affliction or loss of the mind;

11 (139) Or a misfortune dealt by the king;[5] or a dreadful accusation; or a death of a relative; or a loss of treasures;

12 (140) Or a lightning fire that destroys their house. And on the dissolution of their bodies, these fools will go to hellish realms.[6]

13 (141) Not nakedness, not matted locks, not unwashed filth, not fasting, not sleeping on the bare earth, not rubbing the body with dust, not sitting motionless can purify those who have not overcome their doubts about this matter of punishment.[7]

14 (142) Those who, though finely clad, practice tranquility, temperance, equanimity, and self-control, and who do not injure others, are indeed brahmans, ascetics, monks.[8]

15 (143) Is there in the whole world one person so restrained by modesty that he or she needs no reproof, like a horse so excellently trained that it needs no whip?

16 (144) Like a well-trained horse when touched by a whip, be eager and active to do good. By faith, by commitment, by vigor, by attention, by insight into the law,[9] and by virtuous behavior, you will cast off the burden of misery.

17 (145) Irrigators guide the water; fletchers craft the arrow; carpenters shape the wood; good people fashion themselves.

1 See ch. 10, n. 3.

2 The chariot is a famous image used in Buddhism (most notably in the Theravada text *The Questions of King Milinda*) to teach that the self does not exist as an entity unto itself. Just as the concept "chariot" is made up of a transient combination of components—including physical parts, design, assembly, motion, driver, horses, and road—so the concept "self" consists of a temporary combination of five impermanent aggregates (*khanda*; Skt. *skandha*): the body, sensations, perceptions, mental formations, and consciousness.

3 This verse quotes one of the Buddha's most famous speeches, uttered immediately after he attained enlightenment. The "maker of the house" is the self (in the Buddha's case, himself), an artificial construct which gives one the illusion of living a life separate from everything else in the universe. A person who attains enlightenment finally lives beyond this illusion of self, and therefore outside the chain of birth, death, and rebirth.

11 ☐ Old Age

1 (146) How is there laughter, how is there joy, as this world is always burning?[1] Why do you not seek a light, you who are shrouded in darkness?

2 (147) This body is a painted image, covered with wounds, bunched together, sickly, weak, and impermanent.

3 (148) This body is wasting, frail, a nest of disease. This heap of corruption falls to pieces, life ending in death.

4 (149) What happiness can there be for those who see that their white bones will ultimately be cast away like gourds in the autumn?

5 (150) For a while, a house is built around these bones, with a cover of flesh and blood, and within it dwell old age and death, pride and illusion.

6 (151) The brilliant chariots of kings wear away.[2] The health of the body likewise erodes, but the virtue of good people knows not age. Thus do the good themselves testify.

7 (152) One who has learned little grows old like a dumb ox: Flesh may increase, but not wisdom.

8/9 (153/154) Looking for the maker of this house, I ran to no avail through a string of many births, and wearisome is birth again and again. But now, maker of the house, you have been seen. You shall not raise this house again. All the rafters are broken; the ridgepole is shattered. The mind, approaching eternity, has attained the extinction of all desires.[3]

Let me respectfully remind you,
life and death are of supreme importance.
Time swiftly passes by and opportunity is lost.
Each of us should strive to awaken.
Awaken. Take heed.
Do not squander your life.

—The evening gatha as chanted at Zen Mountain Monastery in Mt. Tremper, New York (from *Waking Up: A Week Inside a Zen Monastery*)

10 (155) Those who have not led a spiritual life and have not laid up spiritual treasure in their youth pine away like old herons in a lake without fish.

11 (156) Those who have not lived a spiritual life and have not laid up spiritual treasure in their youth lie around useless like worn-out bows, sighing after the past.

1 Throughout this version of chapter 12, the word "self" is used when it refers to the artificial and problematic sense of separateness that can dominate one's concept of being (for example, in verses 5 and 9). When the suffix "self" occurs in a compound word (for example, "yourself" in verses 1 and 2), it does not carry the same philosophical weight. Instead, it refers in a more practical way to the individual reader.

2 The phrase "three watches of the night" refers to the common military or administrative division of the nighttime (sunset to sunrise) into three equal sections, so that guards or other employees might be relieved at regular intervals. Pali and Sanskrit accounts of the Buddha's overnight enlightenment experience refer to three watches, during which he progressed through various stages of realization.

3 This verse says that the "self" is one's master until one overcomes the notion of "self" by realizing one's true identity—a sense of being that is far more universal and, therefore, much more difficult to locate than "self."

4 The wise ones: *ariyas*, those who are on the path toward enlightenment.

5 The kattaka reed dies shortly after it bears fruit, or else it is cut down for the sake of the fruit as soon as that fruit appears.

12 □ Self

1 (157) If you hold yourself dear, guard yourself carefully.[1] Keep vigil during at least one of the three watches of the night.[2]

2 (158) First direct yourself to what is right, then teach others. Thus the wise do not suffer.

3 (159) If you make yourself as you teach others to be, then, being well guided, you may guide others. One's own self is indeed difficult to subdue.

4 (160) Your own self is your master. Who else could it be? With self well subdued, you gain a master hard to find.[3]

5 (161) The evil done by one's self, born of one's self, suckled by one's self, crushes the foolish including oneself, even as a diamond cuts a stone.

6 (162) Even as a creeping vine overcomes a tree, so the deeds of evil-doers pull them down to a state their enemies would wish for them.

7 (163) Deeds bad for others and ourselves are easy to do. Deeds good for others and ourselves are difficult to do.

8 (164) Foolish ones who scorn the instructions of the wise ones[4] and follow a false doctrine—they bear the fruits of their own destruction, like the kattaka reed.[5]

9 (165) By one's self the evil is done; by one's self one suffers. By one's self evil is left undone; by one's self one is purified.

6 This verse, like the first three verses, emphasizes that it is important to gain mastery over yourself before you attempt to guide or assist someone else. Otherwise, you may unknowingly be doing this person more harm than good. When you do master yourself, you realize your interconnection with everyone else, so that guiding and assisting others becomes a major part of your duty.

If we don't begin with ourselves, we have no way of actually, truly loving others.

—Ayya Khema

To study the Buddha way is to study the self.
To study the self is to forget the self.
To forget the self is to be enlightened by the 10,000 things.

—Zen Master Dogen (from *Waking Up: A Week Inside a Zen Monastery*)

10 (166) Do not forget your duty to yourself for the sake of someone else's need, however great that might be. After you have discerned your own duty, be diligent in fulfilling it.[6]

1 The world: *loka,* meaning the world of everyday reality or relativity, as opposed to the absolute reality of enlightenment.

2 This verse is similar to a famous passage in the *Diamond Sutra,* composed in the fourth century C.E.: "Thus shall you think of all this fleeting world:/A star at dawn, a bubble in a stream;/A flash of lightning in a summer cloud,/A flickering lamp, a phantom, and a dream" (translated by Dr. Kenneth Sanders in *Wisdom of the East*).

3 The full moon is a common symbol of enlightenment in Buddhism. Part of the symbolism involved is that the moon appears in phases. Also, the Buddha reportedly became enlightened on a full-moon night.

4 Their "miraculous power" is their natural ability to fly. Bird flight in general was inexplicable in the Buddha's time and continues to pose mysteries today. Similarly, the human ability to "rise above the world" is paradoxically both miraculous and natural.

5 Mara: see ch. 1, n.4; ch. 20, n. 4.

6 In Buddhism, precepts are vows that one takes up on his or her own to lead a wiser, more compassionate life. They may be embraced by laypeople during a ceremony in which one "takes refuge [in the Buddha, the Dharma, and the Sangha]," or becomes a Buddhist, or by novice monks and nuns in a monastic ordination (see ch. 14, n. 7 for an explanation of Sangha). The number and wording of the precepts varies greatly from school to school, but five basic precepts are common to all Buddhist traditions: (1) Avoid causing harm to other sentient beings; (2) avoid taking anything that is not freely given; (3) avoid sexual misconduct; (4) avoid untruthfulness; and (5) avoid clouding the mind with drugs.

13 □ The World[1]

1 (167) Do not obey evil laws! Do not live on in thoughtlessness! Do not follow false doctrines! Do not be enamored of the world!

2/3 (168/169) Rouse yourself! Do not be idle! Follow the law of virtue! The virtuous rest in bliss in this world and the next.

4 (170) Look upon the world as you would on a bubble. Look upon it as a mirage.[2] The lord of death does not see the one who thus regards the world.

5 (171) Come, look at this world, glittering like a royal chariot. The foolish are immersed in it, but the wise are not attached to it.

6 (172) One who formerly was reckless and afterward became sober brightens up this world like the moon[3] when freed from the clouds.

7 (173) One whose evil deeds are covered by good deeds brightens up this world, like the moon when freed from the clouds.

8 (174) This world is shrouded in darkness. Few can see here. Few go to heaven, like birds escaped from the net.

9 (175) Swans follow the path of the sun. They fly through the ether by means of their miraculous power.[4] Those who are steadfast rise above the world when they conquer Mara[5] and his followers.

10 (176) If one has broken a single precept,[6] if one speaks lies and scoffs at the notion that there can be another world, there is no evil this person will not do.

7 Stingy: those who are selfish, withholding, or otherwise unwilling to sacrifice their own resources or comfort for the good of others. Some Buddhist schools or orders include a precept to avoid stinginess toward others.

In Vajrayana Buddhism, the endless knot symbolizes the endless cycle of rebirth. (Painting by Deepak Chitrakar)

11 (177) The stingy[7] do not go to the world of the gods. Fools only do not praise generosity. A wise one rejoices in generosity, and through it becomes blessed in the other world.

12 (178) Better than gaining sovereignty over Earth, better than ascending to the highest heaven, better than holding lordship over all the worlds, is the reward of the first step taken on the true way.

1 In Sanskrit as well as Pali, *buddha* means "the awakened one." "The Buddha" is an epithet bestowed on the historical teacher Siddhartha Gautama, founder of Buddhism, but the word *buddha* can also refer to anyone who has experienced enlightenment.

2 The word "trackless" connotes the purity of the awakened one's thoughts, words, and deeds. The implication is that such a person leaves behind no "defilements." A well-known injunction in Zen training is, "Leave no traces."

3 True law: *dhamma.* See ch. 1, n. 3.

4 The greatest good: *nibbana* (Skt. *nirvana*). See ch. 2, n. 1. Here the word is translated "the greatest good" because it is used metaphorically, as "heaven" often is in English (e.g., "I was in heaven").

5 "To sleep and sit alone" can be taken literally, as a monastic vow (monks were the primary audience for the Dhammapada at the time it was created), or figuratively, as a more concise means of saying, "to take personal responsibility for one's activities and to do so in a manner that does not interfere with others."

14 □ The Buddha[1]

1 (179) The one who is the conqueror and cannot be conquered, the one whose conquest no one in this world can challenge—by what track can you lead this person: the awakened, the all-seeing, the trackless?[2]

2 (180) The one whom no desire with its snares and poisons can lead astray, by what track can you lead this person: the awakened, the all-seeing, the trackless?

3 (181) Even the gods envy those who are awakened and not forgetful, who are given to meditation, who are wise, and who delight in the repose of retirement from the world.

4 (182) Difficult is it to obtain birth in human form. Difficult is the life of mortals. Difficult is the hearing of the true law;[3] difficult is the attainment of buddhahood.

5 (183) Not to commit any sin, to do only good, and to purify one's mind: That is the teaching of all the awakened.

6 (184) The awakened say that patience is the best kind of penance; self-control, the greatest good.[4] For no one is a holy hermit who oppresses others, no one is an ascetic who insults others.

7 (185) Not to blame, not to strike, to live restrained under the law, to be moderate in eating, to sleep and sit alone,[5] and to dwell on the highest thoughts—that is the teaching of the awakened.

8 (186) There is no satisfying lusts, even by a shower of gold pieces. The one who knows that lusts have a short taste and cause pain wise.

6 Trees were often the object of veneration in ancient India. The Buddha's mother is said to have grabbed the branch of a sacred tree before giving birth to the Buddha, and the Buddha's night of enlightenment was spent sitting beneath a sacred tree, the bo tree.

7 The Buddha, the Dharma (the "truth" or "way," as revealed in the Buddha's teachings), and the Sangha (the community of the Buddha's followers) are known as the Three Jewels.

8 The Four Noble Truths, as revealed during the Buddha's enlightenment, are summarized in the next verse. They are commonly expressed as four statements: (1) All life is suffering; (2) The cause of suffering is desire; (3) Suffering can be ended; (4) The way to end suffering is the Noble Eightfold Path: right understanding, right thought, right speech, right action, right livelihood, right effort, right mindfulness, and right meditation.

Inner refuge is refuge in ourselves, in our ultimate potential. When we recognize and nourish this potential, we have found the real meaning of refuge.

—Kathleen McDonald

9 The meaning here is that the amount or degree of merit is immeasurably great. The statement would seem to criticize the practice of assigning certain measurable amounts or degrees of merit to specific acts.

9 (187) Even in heavenly pleasures this one finds no satisfaction. The disciple who is fully awakened delights only in the destruction of all desires.

10 (188) People driven by fear go to many a refuge—to mountains and forests, to groves and sacred trees.[6]

11 (189) But these are not safe refuges, these are not the best refuges. A person is not delivered from all pains after going to these refuges.

12 (190) The one who takes refuge in the Buddha, the Dharma, and the Sangha;[7] the one who, with clear understanding, sees the Four Noble Truths[8]—

13 (191) Suffering, the origin of suffering, the destruction of suffering, and the Noble Eightfold Path that leads to release from suffering—

14 (192) That is the safe refuge, that is the best refuge. A person is delivered from all pains after going to this refuge.

15 (193) A buddha is not easily found, a buddha is not born everywhere. Wherever such a sage is born, the people around that sage prosper.

16 (194) Happy is the birth of the awakened, happy is the teaching of the true law, happy is peace among the followers of the law, happy is the devotion of those who are at peace.

17/18 (195/196) The one who pays homage to those who deserve homage—whether the buddhas, or their disciples, or those who have overcome the host of evils and crossed the flood of sorrows, the one who pays homage to those who have found deliverance and know no fear, this one's merit can never be measured by anyone.[9]

1 Happiness: *sukkha* (Skt. *suhkha*), the opposite of *dukkha* (Skt. *duhkha*) or "suffering," the main subject of the Four Noble Truths (see ch. 14, n. 8). The meaning here is the state in which one lives when one has ended suffering.

2 The intent in the verse is not to discount compassion for those among us who are ailing physically, emotionally, or spiritually. We are not made happy *because* we are better off than the ones around us. We can only be made happy when we are free from ailments *even though* others around us are not. Contributing to this kind of happiness is the fact that we are then free to help others who are suffering.

3 In this verse, "hunger" and "bodily demands" refer to all those desires or cravings to which we are subject because we exist in human form.

15 □ Ha

1 (197) We live happily indeed when we are not hating those who hate us! Among those who hate us let us dwell free from hatred!

2 (198) We live happily indeed when we are free from ailments among the ailing! Among those who are ailing let us dwell free from ailments![2]

3 (199) We live happily indeed when we are free from greed among the greedy! Among those who are greedy let us dwell free from greed!

4 (200) We live happily indeed when we call nothing our own! We shall be like the bright gods, feeding on happiness!

5 (201) Victory breeds hatred, for the conquered are unhappy. Those who have given up both victory and defeat are content and happy.

6 (202) There is no fire like passion, there is no evil like hatred, there is no pain like this bodily existence, there is no happiness higher than peace.

7 (203) Hunger is the worst of diseases, bodily demands are the greatest of evils.[3] If one knows these things truly, that is nirvana, the highest happiness.

8 (204) Health is the greatest of gifts, contentment is the finest of riches, trust is the best of relationships, nirvana is the highest happiness.

9 (205) The one who has tasted the sweetness of solitude and tranquility

4 The law: *dhamma*. See ch. 1, n. 3.

5 Worthy ones: *ariyas*, those who are on the path toward enlightenment.

Happy is one who knows *samsara* and nirvana are not two.

—Milarepa

Happiness and suffering come from your own mind, not from outside. Your own mind is the cause of happiness; your own mind is the cause of suffering. To obtain happiness and pacify suffering, you have to work within your own mind.

—Lama Zopa Rinpoche

becomes free from fear and free from sin, while drinking in the honey of the law.[4]

10 (206) The sight of worthy ones[5] is good, to live with them is always happiness. If one does not see fools, that person will be truly happy.

11 (207) The one who walks in the company of fools suffers a long way. Company with fools, as with enemies, is always painful. Company with the wise is happiness, like meeting with kinfolk.

12 (208) Therefore one ought to follow the wise, the intelligent, the learned, the much-enduring, the dutiful, the worthy. One ought to follow the good and the wise, as the moon follows the path of the stars.

1 In counterpoint to the positive subject of happiness, or the cessation of suffering, addressed in chapter 15, this chapter addresses the negative subject of pleasure or, in other words, the state associated with getting what one craves or desires.

2 The meaning of this statement is that when you define certain things as pleasant, you are automatically defining certain other things as unpleasant. In both cases, you are "clinging" to an illusion—a distinction that is arbitrary and transitory.

3 This does not mean you cannot value or care for someone or something. In Buddhism, real "love" is becoming one with someone or something, so that you give up the egoistic sense of a separate self. It does not involve creating a dualism of "self" and "other." The latter approach, associated with "desirer" and "object of desire," breeds attachment or clinging, with all the associated potential for pain, abuse, and suffering.

16 □ Pleasure[1]

1 (209) Those who give themselves to vanity and do not give themselves to meditation, forgetting the real aim of life and grasping at pleasure, will in time envy those who have exerted themselves in meditation.

2 (210) Let no one ever cling to what is pleasant and what is unpleasant.[2] Otherwise, not to see what is pleasant is painful, and it is painful to see what is unpleasant.

3 (211) Therefore let no one be attached to anything.[3] Loss of the beloved is evil. Those who are attached to nothing and hate nothing have no fetters.

4 (212) From pleasure comes grief, from pleasure comes fear. The one who is free from pleasure knows neither grief nor fear.

5 (213) From affection comes grief, from affection comes fear. The one who is free from affection knows neither grief nor fear.

6 (214) From lust comes grief, from lust comes fear. The one who is free from lust knows neither grief nor fear.

7 (215) From desire comes grief, from desire comes fear. The one who is free from desire knows neither grief nor fear.

8 (216) From craving comes grief, from craving comes fear. The one who is free from craving knows neither grief nor fear.

9 (217) Those who possess compassion and wisdom, who are just, speak the truth, and take responsibility for themselves—those the world holds dear.

4 This phrase is translated elsewhere as "[one] in whom a desire for the Ineffable has sprung up" (Müller); "[one who] is longing for the infinite nirvana" (Mascaró); and "[one who] longs to know what is hard to know." To call more attention to the distinctions being made here, the annotator's translation uses "aspire" with its more spiritual connotations instead of "desire" or "long for" with their more worldly ones. Also, "oneness with the absolute" is used to contrast more sharply with the dualistic, relative nature of attachments. (For information about the translation used in this book, see p. xxi.)

5 The phrase "heading upstream" is used in Theravada Buddhism to indicate those who are far along the path to enlightenment. Those who have just begun it are said to be "entering the stream."

6 This verse and the next one refer to the doctrine of rebirth and karma (literally, cause and effect). The "other world" is the next life. If one has followed the true law in this life (without actually becoming enlightened, and, therefore, ceasing to be reborn at all), then one will be reborn into a better life or "world." See ch. 1, n. 6; ch. 5, n. 5.

10 (218) Those who aspire to oneness with the absolute,[4] who are peaceful in their minds, and whose thoughts are not bewildered by desires—they are called those who are heading upstream.[5]

11 (219) Relatives, friends, and lovers salute those who have done good and have gone from this world to the other[6]—as kinfolk welcome dear ones on their homecoming.

12 (220) In like manner, one's good works bless one who has done good and has gone from this world to the other—as kinfolk welcome dear ones on their homecoming.

1 Name and form: *nama-rupa*, the everyday phenomenal world, having separate things with their separate names.

2 The "unchangeable place" is the world of the absolute or nirvana, as opposed to the world of the relative or *samsara* (*nama-rupa* in verse 1).

17 □ Anger

1 (221) Let us leave aside anger, let us forsake pride, let us overcome all bondage! No sufferings befall those who are not attached to name and form,[1] and who call nothing their own.

2 (222) The one who holds back rising anger like a rolling chariot—that one I call a real driver. Other people are but holding the reins.

3 (223) Let us overcome anger by love, let us overcome evil by good, let us overcome the greedy by generosity, the liar by truth!

4 (224) Speak the truth; do not yield to anger; give if you are asked, even if you give but a little. By these three steps you will come near the gods.

5 (225) The sages who injure no one and who always control their bodies—they will go to the unchangeable place[2] where they will suffer no more.

6 (226) Those who are ever watchful, who study day and night, and who strive after nirvana—their passions will come to an end.

7 (227) There is an old saying, not just one made up today: "They blame the one who sits silent, they blame the one who speaks much, they blame the one who says little." There is no one in worldly affairs who escapes blame.

8 (228) There never was, there never will be, and there is not now a person blamed all the time or praised all the time.

3 Purest gold: in the original text, "gold from the Jambu river," a river (and region) in India famous at the time for yielding the highest-quality gold.

4 Brahma is the creator in Hindu mythology. In Buddhism, the Hindu gods are not worshiped, but they are treated with respect and often appear in scriptural anecdotes and examples.

5 Buddhism makes frequent reference to the three forms of sin: those of the body, tongue, and mind. The implication in verses 12–14 is that it is just as much a sin to *think* in anger as it is to speak or act in anger.

Aware that anger blocks communication and creates suffering, we are determined to take care of the energy of anger when it arises and to recognize and transform the seeds of anger that lie deep in our consciousness. When anger comes up, we are determined not to do or say anything, but to practice mindful breathing or mindful walking and acknowledge, embrace, and look deeply into our anger. We will learn to look with the eyes of compassion at those we think are the cause of our anger.

—Thich Nhat Hanh (Sixth Mindfulness Training from *Being Peace*)

9/10 (229/230) But the one whom discerning people praise repeatedly day after day as one without fault, one who is wise, intelligent, and compassionate—who would dare to blame this person any more than a coin made of purest gold?[3] Even the gods praise such a person, even Brahma[4] praises this one.

11 (231) Guard against anger of the body,[5] and control your body! Cease committing sins of the body, and practice goodness with your body.

12 (232) Guard against anger of the tongue, and control your tongue! Cease committing sins of the tongue, and practice goodness with your tongue.

13 (233) Guard against anger of the mind, and control your mind! Cease committing sins of the mind, and practice goodness with your mind.

14 (234) The resolute who control body, tongue, and mind are indeed well-controlled.

1 Messengers of death: in the original text, Yama, the Hindu god of death, incorporated into the Buddhist folklore. The implication here (for example, in the statement "You are now like a dried-up leaf") and elsewhere in this chapter is not that the reader is chronologically old and therefore about to die, but that the end of one's life can come at any time (that is, each and every one of us is always as vulnerable to death as a dried-up leaf). This chapter underscores the need for everyone to begin immediately and diligently to prepare for death by taking up the true way propounded in chapter 20.

2 Worthy ones: *ariyas*, those who are on the path toward enlightenment.

3 This verse metaphorically refers to the law of karma: for each cause initiated by the doer, there is an effect realized by the doer.

4 Like the other major world religions—Hinduism, Judaism, Christianity, and Islam—Buddhism evolved in a patriarchal society, and its early sacred texts, like those of the other religions, often reflect a prejudice against women. Here, as in various texts from other religions, women are singled out to be warned against lewdness because, from the perspective of a male-dominant culture, a woman's sexual freedom or impropriety can be especially threatening. In some respects, Buddhism at its beginning through the time of the Pali Canon's creation was freer of this kind of prejudice and more open to women than other contemporary religions were, including Hinduism. For example, Buddhism included orders of nuns and maintained that enlightenment was obtainable by both men and women.

18 □ Impurity

1 (235) You are now like a dried-up leaf. The messengers of Death[1] have come near you. You stand at the threshold of your departure, and you have no provisions for your journey.

2 (236) Make of yourself an island, work hard, practice wisdom! When your impurities are blown away and you are free from guilt, you will enter into the heavenly world of the worthy ones.[2]

3 (237) Your life has come to an end. You are near to Death. There is no resting place for you on the road, and you have no provisions for your journey.

4 (238) Make of yourself an island, work hard, practice wisdom! When your impurities are blown away, and you are free from guilt, you will not enter again into birth and decay.

5 (239) Let those who would be wise blow off their impurities, as a smith blows off the impurities of silver, one by one, little by little, moment by moment.

6 (240) As rust sprung from iron eats into its own source, so do the evil deeds of transgressors bring them to an evil end.[3]

7 (241) The taint of prayers is non-repetition; the taint of houses, non-repair; the taint of a beautiful body, sloth; the taint of a watchful person, lack of vigilance.

8 (242) Lewdness is the taint of women;[4] stinginess, the taint of a benefactor. All evil ways taint in this world and the next.

5 Walkers of the way: *bhikkus* or traveling (and begging) monks in the Buddhist tradition. Babbitt says "mendicants." See ch. 2, n. 6.

6 The implication here is that when we rid ourselves of ignorance, we see the other sins for what they are and therefore are naturally motivated to do away with them.

7 Dig up their own roots: that is, destroy themselves, continuing the metaphor of the fragile plant ("dried-up leaf") begun in the first verse.

8 The subtle meaning of this verse—which, in essence, speaks about minding your own business—is perhaps best conveyed in the poetic paraphrase offered by Thomas Byrom: "You may give in the spirit of light or as you please, but if you care how another man gives or how he withholds, you trouble your quiet endlessly."

9 (243) But there is one taint worse than all the others: Ignorance is the greatest taint. O walkers of the way![5] Throw off that taint and become taintless altogether.[6]

10 (244) Life is easy to live for one who is without shame; bold after the fashion of a crow; a mischief-maker; an insulting, arrogant, and dissolute scoundrel.

11 (245) But life is difficult to live for a modest person, who always aims toward what is pure, who is free from attachment, unassuming, unblemished, and clear-seeing.

12 (246) Those who harm the living, who speak lies, who take what is not given to them, who commit adultery with the mates of others;

13 (247) Those who give themselves up to drinking intoxicating beverages—those people, even in this world, dig up their own roots.[7]

14 (248) O mortal one, know this: The intemperate are in a horrible state. Take care that greed and corruption do not bring you to long-lasting grief.

15 (249) People give of themselves according to their sincere conviction or according to their wanton pleasure. If one frets about the food and drink given by others, one will not attain peace by day or night.[8]

16 (250) The one who destroys that fretting and takes it out by the very root will attain peace by night and day.

17 (251) There is no fire like lust, there is no dart like hatred, there is no snare like folly, there is no torrent like greed.

18 (252) The fault of others is easily perceived, but that of one's self is difficult to perceive. People winnow their neighbors' faults like chaff, but hide their own, as a cheat hides an unlucky cast of the die.

9 The phrase "no true Buddhist monk outside the *sangha* [community of Buddhist followers]" is used here instead of the more literal translation of the original text, "no monk outside the order," which might seem to imply that the only true monk is a Buddhist monk. The sense of the phrase is rather that all those calling themselves "Buddhist monks" must belong to an order of Buddhism and, therefore, follow the same path that all *sangha* members are called to follow.

10 The enlightened ones: *tathagatas*, or "thus-gone" ones, those who have achieved perfection and thus have left the cycle of birth and rebirth. Like *buddha,* the term *tathagata* was bestowed as an epithet upon the founding teacher Siddhartha Gautama after his enlightenment. Here and in verse 21, the term is used collectively to refer to all those who become awakened.

19 (253) If one looks after the faults of others and is always inclined to take offense, one's own evil propensities will grow. Far indeed is such a person from the destruction of those propensities.

20 (254) There is no path through the thin air, no true Buddhist monk outside the *sangha*.[9] The world delights in vanity, the enlightened ones[10] are free from vanity.

21 (255) There is no path through the thin air, no true Buddhist monk outside the *sangha*. Nothing in the everyday world abides, but enlightened ones are never shaken.

1 In the context of Buddhism, the just person is one whose life is firmly established in the dharma or true law. A secular analogy would be a judge or justice who is firmly established in civil law.

2 The true law: *dhamma*. See ch. 1, n. 3.

3 For "sees it instinctively," other translators say "sees it bodily" (Babbitt); "[lives] in harmony with it" (Easwaran); "[one's] work is done rightly" (Mascaró).

4 Elders: *theras* (as in the compound word *Theravada,* or "way of the elders"). Officially, to be called a *thera,* a monk needs to be at least ten years past ordination. However, a *thera* also is one considered to have the positive qualities of character mentioned in the next verse.

5 "Old-in-vain": old without having gained the wisdom or maturity that is the main benefit bestowed by aging.

6 In ancient India, a fine complexion, unmarred by poor diet and hard labor in the outdoor sun, was a worldly sign of wealth, privilege, and/or high status.

19 □ The Just[1]

1/2 (256/257) One is not just if one carries a matter by violence. No, one who discerns both right and wrong, who is learned and guides others not by coercion but properly and virtuously, and one who is guardian of the law and intelligent—that one is called just.

3 (258) People cannot be called wise because they talk a great deal. The person who is patient and free from hatred or fear—that person is truly wise.

4 (259) People cannot be called pillars of the true law[2] because they talk a great deal. Even if a person has heard little of the true law but sees it instinctively[3]—that person is a pillar of the true law, one who never neglects it.

5 (260) People cannot be called elders[4] just because their hair is gray. Their age may be ripe, but they are more rightly called "old-in-vain."[5]

6 (261) The one in whom there is also truth, goodness, gentleness, self-control, and moderation, the one who is steadfast and free from impurity—that one is rightly called an elder.

7 (262) Envious, stingy, deceitful people do not become respectable merely by much talking or by the fineness of their complexion.[6]

8 (263) The one in whom flattering speech and fineness of manner are uprooted—that one, when wise and free from hatred, is rightly called respectable.

9 (264) Not by shaving his head does an undisciplined, lying person

7 *Samana* (Skt. *shamana*) is a contemplative ascetic. The implication here is that one becomes a *samana* not merely by remaining silent outwardly, but by quieting evil desires.

8 *Bhikku:* a homeless, wandering monk who begs for food.

9 Being "beyond merit and demerit" means not living in a dualistic world, where one suffers from the desire to acquire merit and avoid demerit instead of simply "living the law" more confidently, knowledgeably, and naturally.

10 A great one: *ariya,* one on the path toward enlightenment.

11 The bliss of release: release from the cycle of birth, death, and rebirth that breeds suffering.

12 Extinction of desire: *nibbana* (Skt. *nirvana*). See ch. 2, n. 1.

become a monk. Can a person be a monk who is still held captive by desires and greed?

10 (265) The one who always quiets evil whether small or large—that one is called a *samana*[7] because that one has stilled all sinful desire.

11 (266) One is not a *bhikku*[8] simply because one begs for alms, not even if that one has professed all of the true law.

12 (267) The one who is beyond merit and demerit,[9] who lives in purity, who passes through the world with knowledge—that one is truly called a *bhikku*.

13/14 (268/269) One is not a sage because one observes silence if one is also foolish and ignorant; but the one who, weighing the balance, chooses the good and rejects the evil—that person is a sage and for that very reason. The one who understands both alternatives is therefore called a sage.

15 (270) One is not a great one[10] because one defeats or harms other living beings. One is so called because one refrains from defeating or harming other living beings.

16/17 (271/272) Not simply by discipline and vows, nor by much learning, nor by undertaking meditation, nor by sleeping apart do I earn the bliss of release[11] that no worldly person can know. Monk, do not be confident about the way you are living as long as you have not yet attained the extinction of desire.[12]

1 The Noble Eightfold Path is cited in the Four Noble Truths (see n. 2 below) revealed during the Buddha's enlightenment. Its eight parts can be described as: right understanding, right thought, right speech, right action, right livelihood, right effort, right mindfulness, and right meditation.

Easwaran notes that Buddhist scriptures offer little discussion of this path, despite its importance. He explains that it was meant to be conveyed orally—i.e., directly—from teacher to student. Also, as this chapter emphasizes, the way can only be "seen" through personal experience.

2 The Four Noble Truths are commonly expressed as: (1) All life is suffering; (2) The cause of suffering is desire; (3) Suffering can be ended; (4) The way to end suffering is the Noble Eightfold Path.

3 The one who sees: that is, a seer, one with "purity of vision" (see verses 5–7).

4 Mara: the evil being who tried to tempt the Buddha during his enlightenment. Among other tricks, he shot the Buddha with passion-tipped arrows to inflame his sensuality as Mara's daughters danced lasciviously before him. Note the different but related arrow symbol in verse 3.

5 The arrow of suffering: an image in Buddhism (especially prevalent in Tibetan Buddhist art) symbolizing any desire to cling or attach that painfully lodges itself in one's existence. The image implies that any source of suffering needs to be removed swiftly, without prior philosophical consideration, spiritual treatment, or any other form of procrastination. In a famous anecdote in the *Cula Malunkaya Sutta,* the

20 □ The Way

1 (273) The best of paths is the eightfold.[1] The best of truths are the four.[2] The best of mental states is freedom from attachments. The best of human beings is the one who sees.[3]

2 (274) This is the way. There is no other that leads to purity of vision. Go on this way! So shall you confound Mara.[4]

3 (275) If you go on this way, you will make an end of suffering. The way was taught by me after I had understood the removal of the arrow of suffering.[5]

(continued on page 87)

Buddha says, "Suppose a man is wounded by a poisoned arrow and says, 'I will not let this arrow be taken out until I know who shot me, his caste, his family [and so on]....' He would die before he could find out any of these things!"

6 *Tathagatas*: "thus-gone" or "thus-perfected" ones. *Tathagata* is a title referring to the Buddha and, in extension, to any and all enlightened beings.

7 Conditioned things: Pali *samkharas*, phenomena made up of the five conditions or aggregates: matter, sensation, perception, mental formation, and consciousness. The Buddha taught (hence the quotation marks in verse 5) that nothing in the apparently real world exists except as a combination of these aggregates. In other words, nothing has an independent identity of its own.

8 All states: In many translations, the Pali phrase *sabbe dhamma* is translated "all conditioned things" to continue the parallelism of the preceding two verses (a rhetorical device for emphasis). But as Rahula points out, "the word *dhamma* is much wider than *samkhara*. It includes not only the conditioned things..., but also the non-conditioned, the Absolute, Nirvana. There is nothing in the universe or outside, good or bad, conditioned or non-conditioned, relative or absolute, which is not included in this term."

9 Three courses of action: speech, mind, and body. In Buddhist liturgy, these are the three agents that give form to the three poisons of greed, anger, and ignorance. For example, in the Japanese Zen *fusatsu* (renewal of vows) ceremony, monastics declare atonement for all evil committed "because of greed, anger, and ignorance born of my body, mouth, and thought."

10 Meditation: Pali *bhavana,* which can also refer to a specific meditation program rather than simply to meditation. Hence, some translations read "meditative practices" or even "spiritual yoga" (in Sanskrit, *yoga* means "discipline" or "practice").

4 (276) You yourself must make the effort. The *tathagatas*[6] are only teachers. Meditators who enter the way are freed from the bondage of Mara.

5 (277) "All conditioned things[7] are impermanent." The one who knows and perceives this fact ceases to be miserable. This is the way to purity of vision.

6 (278) "All conditioned things are involved in suffering." The one who knows and perceives that fact ceases to be miserable. This is the way to purity of vision.

7 (279) "All states are selfless and unreal."[8] The one who knows and perceives that fact ceases to be miserable. This is the way to purity of vision.

8 (280) One who does not arise when it is time to arise, who is full of sloth though vital and strong, who is weak in will and thought—that lazy and idle one will never find the way to wisdom.

9 (281) Watching speech and carefully restraining the mind, let one never commit any wrong with the body. Let one but keep these three courses of action[9] clear, and one will achieve the way taught by the wise.

10 (282) Through meditation,[10] wisdom is won. Through lack of meditation, wisdom is lost. Let one who knows this two-way path of win and loss behave so that wisdom may be gained.

(continued on page 89)

11 On one level, this statement can refer to doing a complete job in ridding oneself of clinging desires, rather than just a partial one. Thomas Cleary points out another interpretation according to traditional Buddhist symbolism: "The classic Zen master Baizhang said, 'The forest symbolizes mind, the tree symbolizes the body. Fear is aroused because of talk about the forest, so it is said, 'Chop the forest, not the tree.' This underscores the point that Buddhist abstinence and renunciation do not mean torturing the body but rather clearing the mind."

12 Free: You will attain enlightenment.

13 This verse was originally addressed only to monks, and so it represented a direct plea for celibacy. However, as applied to laypeople today, it is not meant to imply that men should give up or separate themselves from women (or vice versa). Instead, the issue is not harboring *lust* for them. Throughout the Dhammapada, one is warned against "attachment" of this kind, meaning any passion-based desire to cling, because it inevitably breeds suffering. For a similar warning, see verse 15. As distinct from lust, which implies an individual self and a separate other (attacher-attachee), true love involves selflessly, compassionately, and wisely becoming one with the beloved and everything else one encounters in the universe.

14 Uprooting a lotus in autumn: that is, weeding out a plant that is dead or dying by autumn.

15 The Happy One: Pali *Sugata,* one of the Buddha's epithets. The word connotes both joy and blessedness.

16 Nirvana: Pali *nibbana,* literally "extinction"; variously interpreted as the end of suffering; release from the cycle of birth and death into an entirely different, higher mode of being; or enlightenment. It should not be confused with the word "death" in the rest of this chapter, which is used to refer to the end of a physical lifetime.

17 The daydreaming fool of this verse is obviously obsessed with material comfort in the world of time and events—a preoccupation that keeps him or her from pursuing the way in this lifetime before it is too late. In India, the monsoon season is late summer.

18 Children are no help…: that is, no help in finding the way.

11 (283) Cut down the whole forest, not one tree only![11] Danger comes out of the forest. When you have cut down the forest and its undergrowth, then you will be free![12]

12 (284) So long as a man's lust for a woman is not overcome, so long is his mind in bondage, as the suckling calf is bound to its nursing mother.[13]

13 (285) Cut out the love of self, like uprooting a lotus in autumn with your hand![14] Cherish the road of peace. The Happy One[15] has shown the way to nirvana.[16]

14 (286) "Here I shall dwell during the monsoon season, here in winter, here in early summer."[17] Thus the fool fancies and does not think of death.

15 (287) Death comes and carries off the one whose mind is wholly caught up in children and possessions, as a flood carries off a sleeping village.

16 (288) Children are no help, nor a parent, nor other relations.[18] There is no help from kinfolk for one whom Death has seized.

17 (289) One who is wise and good and knows the meaning of what is said here should quickly clear the way to nirvana.

1 True brahman: one who is the "highest" person he or she can be in a spiritual sense, as opposed to the traditional Hindu concept of the brahman as a member of the highest social caste (namely, the priestly one). The next highest social caste is that of the warrior. The verse as a whole means that one can overcome even great sins—that is, change the karmic flow in one's life—by following the way of the Buddha.

2 The phrase "kings of the priestly caste" is used here instead of the original "brahman kings" to avoid confusion with "true brahman," and to parallel "warrior caste" in verse 5.

Two of the sins named in verse 6 are nominally even greater than the corresponding ones mentioned in the previous verse. The kings are members of a higher caste, and "a man on the true path" (*ariya*, "worthy one"; see ch. 2, n. 2) is more advanced spiritually than a "kingdom with all of its subjects."

3 The use of "Gautama" here, the family (clan) name of the historical figure called "the Buddha," emphasizes that such disciples follow the teachings of a human being, not a god. The contrasting use of the title "the Buddha" later in this verse indicates that the disciple's mind is set on this individual not as a human being or a god, but as a symbol of enlightenment.

21 □ Miscellany

1 (290) If by leaving a small pleasure one sees a great pleasure, let a wise person leave the small pleasure and look to the great.

2 (291) Those who, by causing pain to others, wish to obtain pleasure for themselves—they, entangled in the bonds of hatred, will never be free from hatred.

3 (292) What they ought to do is neglected, what they ought not to do is done. The desires of unruly, thoughtless people are always increasing.

4 (293) But the people whose whole watchfulness is always on guard against the evils of the body, who do not do what ought not to be done, and who consistently do what ought to be done—the harmful desires of such vigilant and wise people will come to an end.

5 (294) A true brahman goes through life unharmed and is free from sorrow and remorse, even though such a one may have killed father and mother and two kings of the warrior caste, even though such a one has destroyed a kingdom with all its subjects.[1]

6 (295) A true brahman goes through life unharmed and is free from sorrow and remorse, even though such a one may have killed father and mother and two kings of the priestly caste[2] and a man on the true path besides.

7 (296) The disciples of Gautama[3] are always well awake, and their thoughts day and night are always set on the Buddha.

4 The basic meaning of this verse is: Living in the cycle of birth, death, and rebirth always involves suffering, whether you separate yourself from people, live interactively among people, or live a solitary life among people; therefore, you should step out of this cycle (by attaining enlightenment) and, in doing so, end all possibility of suffering.

5 With true glory and treasure: that is, one who is celebrated and rich not in the worldly sense (the common recipient of honor) but in the spiritual one.

6 The perpetually snow-covered peaks of the Himalaya Mountains, which extend across into northern India, are radiantly visible for long distances on clear days, thanks to the reflected sunlight.

7 On the outskirts of the forest: the outer margins of human society, as the forest symbolizes the nonhuman wilderness (the animal kingdom).

8 (297) The disciples of Gautama are always well awake, and their thoughts day and night are always set on the Dharma.

9 (298) The disciples of Gautama are always well awake, and their thoughts day and night are always set on the Sangha.

10 (299) The disciples of Gautama are always well awake, and their thoughts day and night are always set on guarding against the evils of their body.

11 (300) The disciples of Gautama are always well awake, and their minds day and night always delight in compassion.

12 (301) The disciples of Gautama are always well awake, and their minds day and night always delight in meditation.

13 (302) Hard is the life of a hermit—hard to enjoy. The life of one who lives in the world is also difficult and burdensome. And it is painful to live in the world and yet have no like companion. The life of anyone who travels from world to world is filled with suffering. Therefore, one should not be such a wayfarer, and then one will not have to suffer.[4]

14 (303) Wherever goes one who is faithful and virtuous with true glory and treasure,[5] there is that one held in honor.

15 (304) Good people shine from afar, like the peaks of the Himalayas.[6] Bad people are dark and unremarkable even up close, like arrows shot by night.

16 (305) Those who can sit alone, sleep alone, and walk alone without getting weary—those who can subdue themselves all on their own—they will find delight on the outskirts of the forest.[7]

1 According to Buddhist doctrine, "hell" is experienced in the context of the next lifetime and not necessarily any longer than that (assuming the individual changes the direction of his or her karmic flow).

2 The next world: the next lifetime, which, in the case of an evil person, would be spent in one of the hellish realms.

According to the doctrine of karma as it relates to rebirth, the overall quality of one's life—and especially one's state of mind just before death—sets in motion the next lifetime. However, once one has entered that next lifetime, he or she can begin a positive shift in the chain of cause and effect (karma). Accordingly, this verse reads "people who *have done* evil deeds" instead of "people who *do* evil deeds."

3 People whose shoulders...: Buddhist monks (who typically wear yellow robes).

4 The phrase "uncomfortable bed" is a metaphor for troubled sleep. In this verse, the point is made that an evil person experiences hell in this life, too, as well as the next life (assuming his or her evil ways don't change). Hell in this life manifests itself both psychologically and socially.

5 "Badly practiced asceticism" covers a wide range of behaviors, as the remainder of the chapter indicates. Most pointedly it refers to undertaking extreme austerities or self-mortifications for their own sake, assuming that such acts alone make one worthy. In Buddhist terms, it is better to pursue a more thoughtful "middle way" of self-control, doing what is necessary and not doing what is not necessary.

22 □ The Downward Course

1 (306) The one who says what is not goes to hell.[1] So does the one who, having done a thing, says, "I have not done it." After death both are equal. In the next world, they are people who have done evil deeds.[2]

2 (307) Many people whose shoulders are covered with the yellow robe[3] are of bad character and lack self-control. Such evildoers by their evil deeds go to hell.

3 (308) Better it would be to swallow an iron ball as hot as a flaring fire than to live as a bad, unrestrained person on the charity of the land.

4 (309) Four things befall the heedless one who pursues a neighbor's spouse—first, acquisition of demerit; second, an uncomfortable bed;[4] third, evil report; and, fourth and lastly, hell.

5 (310) There is acquisition of demerit and the downward course to hell; there is the short pleasure of the frightened in the arms of the frightened; and the imposition by the king of heavy punishment. Therefore, let no one's desirous thoughts turn to a neighbor's spouse.

6 (311) As a grass blade, if badly grasped, cuts the hand, so badly practiced asceticism[5] leads to hell.

7 (312) An act carelessly performed, a broken vow, and a wavering obedience to religious discipline—all these things bear no great fruit.

6 Dust, an especially problematic physical phenomenon in India, is an image often used in Buddhism for spiritual defilements—things a person thinks, says, or does that are not wise or compassionate and, therefore, that dirty his or her essential purity. In Zen, the act of seated meditation (zazen) is sometimes described as "polishing dust from the mirror."

7 The good path: *dhammapada,* the path of the dharma, as opposed to the "downward course" to hell, the lowest realm of existence.

8 (313) If anything ought to be done, let one do it, and do it vigorously! A lax ascetic only scatters the dust of defilement more widely.[6]

9 (314) An evil deed is better left undone, for one feels remorse for it afterward. A good deed is better done, for having done it, one does not feel remorse.

10 (315) Like a well-guarded frontier fort, having defenses within and without, guard yourself. Not a moment should escape attention, for those who allow the right moment to pass suffer pain when they are in hell.

11 (316) Those who are ashamed of what they ought not to be ashamed of, and are not ashamed of what they ought to be ashamed of—such people, embracing false doctrines, enter the downward course.

12 (317) Those who fear when they ought not to fear, and fear not when they ought to fear—such people, embracing false doctrines, enter the downward course.

13 (318) Those who see sin where none exists, and do not see sin where it does exist—such people, embracing false doctrines, enter the downward course.

14 (319) Those who know what is forbidden as forbidden, and what is not forbidden as what is not forbidden—such people, embracing the true doctrine, enter the good path.[7]

1 The elephant, king of animals in Indian folklore, is also a common symbol of endurance and trainability. The Buddha himself was called "the Great Elephant." In this chapter the Pali word *danta,* meaning "trained" or "self-restrained," is repeatedly played against the word *danti,* one of many words meaning "elephant."

2 The untrodden country: nirvana, the great emptiness or oneness where no distinctions are made.

3 Dhanapalaka (Pali, "Treasure Guardian") is a popular character in Indian folklore. In this verse, he is described as being in rut, or filled with lust. This verse and the next one list various states characterized by a lack of self-control.

4 In this verse, we see a rare use of the first person, referring to the Buddha himself. Throughout the Dhammapada, certain verses seem to have been recast over time into the third person: they refer to "the Buddha" as if the Buddha himself were not the author. The use of the first person becomes more frequent from here on in the text, an appropriate device to lend authority to the conclusion.

Here the Buddha alludes to his past existence as a pampered, self-indulgent prince. His father, King Suddhodana, surrounded him with every possible luxury to predispose him to become a great king instead of a spiritual leader, as prophesied.

5 The phrase "happy but considerate" is used to distinguish proper joyfulness from mindless self-satisfaction.

23 □ The Elephant[1]

1 (320) Patiently shall I endure abuse as the elephant in battle endures the arrow sent from the bow, for the world is ill-natured.

2 (321) They lead a trained elephant to battle. The king mounts a trained elephant. The trained person is the best among humans, the one who patiently endures abuse.

3 (322) Mules are good if trained, and so are noble horses and great elephants, but humans who train themselves are better still.

4 (323) For riding these animals, no human reaches the untrodden country.[2] One must go there upon one's own, well-tamed self.

5 (324) The elephant called Dhanapalaka, his temples running with musk, is difficult to restrain and will not eat. Instead, he longs to mate in the elephant grove.[3]

6 (325) If a person becomes lazy and a great eater, if a person is sleepy and rolls around like a great hog fed on wash—that fool is born again and again.

7 (326) This mind of mine went formerly wandering about as it liked, as it listed, as it pleased, but I shall now hold it in firmly, as the rider who wields the hook holds in the furious elephant.[4]

8 (327) Be not thoughtless, watch your thoughts! Draw yourself out of the evil way, like an elephant sunk in mud.

9 (328) If you find a prudent companion who walks with you, is wise, and lives soberly, it is well to walk with this companion, overcoming all dangers, happy but considerate.[5]

6 Here and in the next two verses, the word "pleasant" refers to something that is properly agreeable, in a spiritual sense, as is described in verse 9: "[a companion who is] happy but considerate."

The elephant, a symbol of endurance and trainability, has an honored spot in Buddhist legend. The Buddha's mother dreamed that a white elephant entered her womb, foretelling his birth, and the Buddha himself is sometimes called "the Great Elephant." (Painting by Kiran Chitrakar)

10 (329) If you find no prudent companion who walks with you, is wise, and lives soberly, walk alone, like a king who has left his conquered country behind, like an elephant in the forest.

11 (330) In such a case it is better to live alone. There is no companionship with a fool. Walk alone, commit no sin, have few wishes, like an elephant in the forest.

12 (331) If the occasion arises, friends are pleasant.[6] Enjoyment is pleasant, whatever the cause may be. A good deed is pleasant in the hour of death. The giving up of all grief is pleasant.

13 (332) Pleasant in the world is the state of a mother, pleasant the state of a father, pleasant the state of an ascetic, pleasant the state of a brahman.

14 (333) Pleasant is virtue lasting to old age, pleasant is a faith firmly rooted, pleasant is attainment of intelligence, pleasant is avoiding of sins.

1 Thirst: *tanha* (Skt. *trishna*), commonly used to mean "craving" or "desire" in general, the root of all suffering. India being a very hot country, thirst was an especially appropriate choice to represent craving to the early Indian followers of the Buddha.

In the Theravada scripture *Samyutta Nikaya,* the Buddha speaks of three different kinds of desire: the desire for sensory pleasure (the primary one discussed in this chapter); the desire for life (i.e., clinging to this world of suffering); and the desire for extinction (i.e., clinging to the hope of nirvana).

The last kind of desire is perhaps the most difficult to accept as negative. The point is a subtle one: namely, that even clinging to the pursuit of nirvana results in suffering and bondage. Instead of desiring nirvana in a craven way (for example, as a self-serving achievement or a spiritual goal), one should aspire to realizing nirvana as a natural extension of one's own true wisdom and compassion.

2 Birana grass, especially tough and fast-growing, is considered a weed by Indian farmers.

3 The lotus, a beautiful water lily that grows in the mud, is a symbol in Buddhism for the true, inner perfection of each human being, even though he or she lives in a world of corruption.

4 Mara: the archetypal tempter (see ch. 1, n. 4). The usira root is especially fragrant and is used for making tea and incense.

5 The thirty-six channels: the variety of possible sensual experiences that can breed suffering. In Buddhism, there are six main categories of sensual experience (related organs in parentheses): seeing (eyes), hearing (ears), smelling (nose), tasting (tongue), touching (body), and thinking (mind). These categories can both build on themselves and interweave with each other, hence six times six equals thirty-six.

24 □ Thirst[1]

1 (334) The thirst of a thoughtless person grows like a creeper. That person runs from life to life, like a monkey seeking fruit in the forest.

2 (335) Whoever is overcome by this fierce, poisonous thirst—in this world, that person's sufferings increase like the abounding birana grass.[2]

3 (336) But whoever overcomes this fierce, poisonous thirst—in this world, that person is difficult to be conquered, and that person's sufferings fall off like water dropping from a lotus leaf.[3]

4 (337) This salutary counsel I give you: "Dig up the root of thirst, as a person who wants the sweet-scented usira root must dig up the birana grass, so that Mara[4] may not crush you again and again, as the stream crushes the reeds."

5 (338) As a cut-down tree grows up again as long as its main root is sound and firm, even so will pain return again and again if your proneness to thirst is not destroyed.

6 (339) Those misguided ones whose thirst, running toward pleasure, is exceedingly strong in the thirty-six channels[5]—such ones will be swept away by waves, namely, their own desires that incline to lust.

7 (340) The currents run in all directions, the creeper keeps on sprouting. If you see the creeper springing up, cut its roots by means of wisdom.

❖ Desires achieved increase thirst like salt water.

—Milarepa

6 Wandering monks: *bhikkus*, ordained monks who live a life of homelessness and begging.

7 The craving for a spouse and children breeds suffering. Instead of craving such individuals as possessions, one should join in these relationships (if life presents the opportunity) free of clinging expectations, needs, fears, and desires.

8 The meaning of this verse is as follows: In nirvana ("the other shore of existence"), time—the world of birth, suffering, and death—doesn't exist. All is one. Therefore one must cease separating experience into different categories, such as "ahead" (future), "behind" (past), and "between" (present).

8 (341) A misguided creature's pleasures are extravagant and luxurious. Sunk in lust and keen on happiness, people undergo birth and decay again and again.

9 (342) Those driven by thirst run around like hunted hares. Held in fetters and bonds of their own, they undergo long-lasting pain again and again.

10 (343) Those driven by lust run about like hunted hares. Therefore, let wandering monks[6] who desire to be free from lust first conquer their thirst.

11 (344) Those who, having broken free from lust, give themselves up to lust again—those who, having escaped the jungle, run back to the jungle—these ones are caught in bondage.

12 (345) Wise people do not call a fetter strong that is made of iron, wood, or hemp. A far stronger fetter is the desperate craving for precious stones and rings, for a spouse and children.[7]

13 (346) Wise people call the bond strong that drags one wholly downward and though capable of yielding is very difficult to undo. After having cut this bond at last, people leave this world free from cares and free from sensual cravings.

14 (347) Those who are slaves to passion follow the stream of desires, as a spider runs down the web it has made. When they have ceased to do this, at last they make true progress, free from cares and leaving all pains behind.

15 (348) Give up what is ahead, give up what is behind, give up what is between, when you go to the other shore of existence.[8] If your mind is altogether free, you will not again enter into birth and decay.

16 (349) If you allow yourself to be tossed by doubts and swayed by strong passions, and if you yearn only for what is sensually pleasing,

9 The thorns of life: one's "clingings," whether one is doing the clinging or being clung to. People who have abandoned clinging are eligible for entry into nirvana, or the absolute, and, therefore, escape from *samsara,* or the cycle of birth, death, and rebirth. Such a person will not be reborn into another body.

10 Those who know the proper order of things: in Müller's translation, "who know the order of letters (those which are before and which are after)." Great sages are those who are not confused, misled, or ignorant about even the smallest details (the letters used in the words of the teachings).

11 The true law: *dhamma*. See ch. 1, n. 3.

12 The other shore: nirvana. See ch. 2, n. 1.

13 The "gift" here can be interpreted in two ways. It can refer to the true law *(dhamma),* as defined in verse 21, in which case the meaning is that the true law is especially rewarding for those who are free from greed.

Alternatively, it can refer to *any* offering one individual makes out of respect or compassion to another individual who is free from greed. In this case, the meaning is that such an offering brings great reward to the giver, presumably because the giver has done the right thing.

your thirst will grow greater and greater, and you will make your bonds stronger and stronger.

17 (350) If you cultivate delight in quieting doubts and, always reflecting, dwell on what is not just sensually pleasing, you certainly will remove, nay, cut through the fetters of Mara.

18 (351) Those who have reached the consummation, who do not fear, who are without thirst and without sin—these people have broken off all the thorns of life; the body they have will be their last.[9]

19 (352) Those who are without thirst and without attachment, who understand the true teachings and their proper interpretation, who know the proper order of things[10]—these people have received their last body, are called great sages, are called great human beings.

20 (353) I have overcome all, I know all. In all conditions of life, I am free from taint. I have ceased all clinging; and through the destruction of thirst, I am free. Having learned for myself, whom should I indicate as my teacher?

21 (354) The gift of the true law exceeds all gifts.[11] The sweetness of the true law exceeds all sweetness. The delight offered by the true law exceeds all delights. The extinction of thirst overcomes all pain.

22 (355) Riches destroy the foolish, not those who seek the other shore.[12] The foolish destroy themselves and others by their thirst for riches.

23 (356) Fields are damaged by weeds, people are damaged by greed. Therefore, a gift[13] bestowed on those who are free from greed brings great reward.

24 (357) Fields are damaged by weeds, people are damaged by anger.

White Tara represents universal compassion, helping others to cross the ocean of existence and suffering to happiness. Her seven eyes (on her forehead, hands, and feet) symbolize the vigilance of her compassion, her right hand makes a boon-granting gesture, and her left hand holds a lotus and is in a position that indicates protection. Her white color signifies purity and truth, which is complete and undifferentiated. (Painting by Madhu and Sangita Chitrakar)

Therefore, a gift bestowed on those who are free from anger brings great reward.

25 (358) Fields are damaged by weeds, people are damaged by delusion. Therefore, a gift bestowed on those who are free from delusion brings great reward.

26 (359) Fields are damaged by weeds, people are damaged by craving. Therefore, a gift bestowed on those who are free from craving brings great reward.

1 The monk: *bhikku* (Skt. *bhikshu*). Specifically, the term means a fully ordained and homeless male monk who wanders from place to place, teaching and begging as he goes along. The female equivalent is *bhikkuni* (Skt. *bhikshuni*). During the Buddha's lifetime and long afterward, all ordained monks were *bhikku*s. Eventually, most orders housed monks permanently in monasteries, although such monks might still wander and beg on a regular or occasional basis.

In the context of the Dhammapada, we may consider the title of this chapter as referring both to ordained monks and to true monks at heart, whether they are ordained or not—that is, the type of people who are on their way to nirvana. In acknowledgment of this latter, more Western-friendly meaning, Byrom titles this chapter "The Seeker."

2 The true law: the *dhamma*. See ch. 1, n. 3.

3 Name and form: *nama-rupa,* that is, the world of transitory things that have differing names and forms.

25 □ The Monk[1]

1 (360) Restraint in the eye is good, good is restraint in the ear; in the nose restraint is good, good is restraint in the tongue;

2 (361) In the body restraint is good, good is restraint in speech; in thought restraint is good, good is restraint in all things. A monk restrained in all things is free from suffering.

3 (362) Those who control their hands, those who control their feet, those who control their speech, those who are well controlled, those who delight inwardly, those who are collected, those who are solitary and content—let them be called monks.

4 (363) Monks who control their mouths, who speak wisely and calmly, who teach the meaning of the true law[2]—their words are sweet.

5 (364) The monk who dwells in the true law, delights in the true law, meditates on the true law, recollects the true law—that monk will never fall away from the true law.

6 (365) Let monks not devalue what they have received, nor ever envy others: A monk who envies others does not obtain peace of mind.

7 (366) Monks who, though receiving little, do not devalue what they have received—even the gods will praise them if their lives are pure and if they are not slothful.

8 (367) Those who never identify themselves with name and form[3] and do not grieve over what is no more—those ones indeed are rightly called monks.

4 The quiet place: nirvana. See ch. 2, n. 1.

5 The word "boat" is used as a metaphor for one's worldly (gross) being, which includes the six senses (eye, ear, nose, tongue, body, and mind). In Zen this aggregate is commonly called the "skin bag," the phenomenon we erroneously think of as our separate, distinct self.

6 In this verse, the four categories of "five," apparently referring to various Buddhist doctrines, are identified variously by commentators. The first three explanations below derive primarily from those given by Thomas Cleary, who offers an especially concise description of the most common and convincing identifications.

- "cut off five": the five lower or cruder bonds, which require harsh measures to break—desire, aggression, belief in the body as real, cultic ritualism, and vacillation.
- "renounce five": the five higher or more subtle bonds, which can more easily be broken by force of will—greed in respect to worldly matters; greed in respect to spiritual matters; excitement; conceit; and ignorance in respect to spiritual matters.
- "rise above five": the five bonds of hell ("the downward course") which need to be transcended—lust, anger, folly, pride, and prejudice.
- "the five fetters": a phrase that collectively refers to each and all of the previous groups of five.

Once an individual has overcome these bonds, he or she can be said to have "crossed the flood" or reached nirvana (the "other shore" as opposed to this worldly existence).

7 Swallow the hot iron ball: that is, dwell in hell, the possible consequence for an evildoer in the next lifetime. According to Buddhist mythology, every bit of food or drink consumed in hell goes down like a hot iron ball.

8 Those in touch with the immortal: knowledgeable about the undying, absolute realm of truth.

9 (368) Monks who behave with kindness, who are happy in the doctrines of the Buddha, will reach the quiet place[4] and will find happiness arising from the cessation of bodily existence.

10 (369) O monk, bail out this boat![5] If emptied it will go quickly; having cut off lust and hatred, you will reach nirvana.

11 (370) Cut off five, renounce five, rise above five! A monk who has escaped from the five fetters is called "one who has crossed the flood."[6]

12 (371) Meditate, O monk, and take heed! Do not set your heart on sensual pleasures or else for your heedlessness you may have to swallow the hot iron ball[7] and cry out in the midst of fire, "What pain!"

13 (372) Without wisdom there is not meditation, without meditation there is no wisdom. The one who is both meditative and wise is near to nirvana.

14 (373) A monk who with tranquil mind has chosen to live in a bare cell knows an unearthly delight in gaining a clearer and clearer perception of the true law.

15 (374) As soon as such monks have grasped the origin and passing away of the elements of the body, they attain the happiness and joy that belong to those in touch with the immortal.[8]

(continued on page 115)

9 The precepts: see ch. 13, n. 6.

10 As applied to a monk, the phrase "live in charity" has a double meaning: (1) rely on the goodness of others for one's existence; and (2) be charitable oneself.

11 In Buddhism, the full moon is a symbol of enlightenment. See ch. 13, n. 3.

Tibetan Buddhist Monk with begging bowl
(Painting by Madhu and Sangita Chitrakar)

16 (375) And this is the beginning for noble monks: watchfulness over the senses, contentment, and restraint under the precepts.[9] Let them keep noble friends whose lives are pure and who are not slothful;

17 (376) Let them live in charity,[10] and let them be perfect in their behavior. Then, in fullness of delight, they will make an end of suffering.

18 (377) As the jasmine sheds its withered flowers, even so, O monks, people should shed lust and hatred.

19 (378) The monk whose body, tongue, and mind are quieted, who is collected, and who has rejected the baits of the world—that monk is rightly called quiet.

20 (379) Rouse yourself by yourself, examine yourself by yourself! Thus, self-protected and attentive, you will live happily, O monk!

21 (380) For self is the lord of self, self is the refuge of self. Therefore, curb yourself as the merchant curbs a noble horse.

22 (381) The monk who is full of delight in the doctrines of the Buddha will reach the quiet place and will find happiness consisting in the cessation of bodily existence.

23 (382) Monks who, even when young, apply themselves to the doctrines of the Buddha brighten up this world, like the moon when free from the clouds.[11]

1 The Brahman: a member of the highest social caste in Hindu India, the priestly one; thus by implication a brahman is considered to be the most highly evolved human being.

Here, the Buddha is redefining "brahman" to reflect what he considers to be truly the most spiritually advanced kind of human being. Thomas Byrom titles this chapter "The True Master."

2 Stop the stream: that is, the ongoing flow of desires.

3 This sentence may be understood as follows: When you've understood that everything created in this world comes to an end, you will also understand that which lies beyond the world of creation and destruction, in other words, nirvana, where nothing is "made" or "destroyed."

4 The other shore: nirvana. See ch. 2, n. 1.

5 One for whom there is neither this nor that shore, nor both: that is, one who does not think in terms of dualisms or separate parts but who rather grasps the absolute, undifferentiated nature of reality.

6 Here the word *Buddha* is meant to be taken two ways: first, as the historical Buddha, Siddhartha Gautama; and second, as any person who has experienced enlightenment and therefore deserves the title *buddha,* meaning "awakened one."

7 Religious recluse: *pabbajita,* the title bestowed upon a Buddhist monk who chooses to live in solitude. Here the meaning is more symbolic.

26 □ The Brahman[1]

1 (383) Stop the stream[2] valiantly, drive away the desires, O brahmans! When you have understood the destruction of all that was made, you will understand that which was not made.[3]

2 (384) If brahmans reach the other shore[4] with insight, self-restraint, and contemplation, all bonds will vanish from them because of the knowledge they have obtained.

3 (385) The one for whom there is neither this nor that shore, nor both—such a one, fearless and unshackled, I call indeed a brahman.[5]

4 (386) Whoever is meditative, blameless, settled, dutiful, free from passions—whoever has attained the highest way—such a one I call indeed a brahman.

5 (387) The sun is bright by day, the moon shines by night. The brahman is bright in meditation, but the Buddha,[6] the Awakened One, is bright with splendor day and night.

6 (388) Because people have put away their own evil, they are therefore properly called brahmans. Because they walk quietly, they are therefore properly called ascetics. Because they have banished their own impurities, they are therefore properly called religious recluses.[7]

7 (389) No one should attack a brahman, but no brahman, if attacked, should fly out at the aggressor! Woe to the one who strikes a brahman! More woe to the brahman who strikes an aggressor!

8 (390) Measure by measure, brahmans are rewarded for holding back

8 A traditional brahman—that is, a Hindu priest—makes sacrifices using fire.

9 Matted locks, robes of antelope skin, and a clean exterior are attributes commonly associated with the traditional brahmans who function as Hindu priests.

their minds from the allurements of life. And in direct proportion as their wish to injure declines, so is their suffering quieted.

9 (391) I call a person a brahman who does not offend by deed, word, or thought and is well controlled in these three respects.

10 (392) The person from whom you have learned the true law as taught by the Buddha—that one you should reverence profoundly, even as the brahman worships the sacrificial fire.[8]

11 (393) People do not become brahmans by virtue of their matted locks, their lineage, or their birth. Those in whom there is truth and righteousness—they are blessed, they are brahmans.

12 (394) What is the use of your matted locks, O fool, of what avail is your robe of antelope skin, if deep within you lurk filthy desires despite your clean exterior?[9]

13 (395) Those who wear cast-off rags, who are emaciated so you can see their veins, who meditate alone in the forest—these people I call indeed brahmans.

14 (396) I do not call people brahmans because of their background or their parents. People attached to such things are indeed arrogant and likely to be rich in a worldly way. But poor ones who are free from such attachments—these people I call indeed brahmans.

15 (397) The ones I call indeed brahmans who, after cutting all fetters, never tremble but stand free and clear.

16 (398) The ones I call indeed brahmans who, after removing all straps, thongs, and ropes, and all the baggage pertaining to those things, are unimpeded and awakened.

17 (399) The ones I call indeed brahmans who, though innocent of offense, endure reproaches, strikes, and bonds—who have patience as their force and strength as their army.

10 Who have received their last body: that is, who have, in this lifetime, transcended the cycle of birth, death, and rebirth, so that they are eligible at death to enter nirvana instead of being reborn. Thus the body they now have is their last one.

11 A mustard seed, used as a spice or an ingredient in sauces or medicines, is dug out of the plant with a needle. See also verse 25.

12 The implication here is that one should not cling to the society of laypeople and/or monks as a means of defining or exercising one's own identity. A true spiritual master is one who attains enlightenment on his or her own.

18 (400) The ones I call indeed brahmans who are free from anger, dutiful, virtuous, temperate, and self-controlled—who have received their last body.[10]

19 (401) The ones I call indeed brahmans who do not cling to sensual pleasures, like water on a lotus leaf, like a mustard seed on the point of a needle.[11]

20 (402) The ones I call indeed brahmans who, even in this world, know the end of their own suffering—who have put down their burden and are unencumbered.

21 (403) The ones I call indeed brahmans whose knowledge is deep and who are wise as well—who know the right way and the wrong way and have attained the highest end

22 (404) The ones I call indeed brahmans who keep independent both from laypeople and monks—who wander alone and have few desires.[12]

23 (405) The ones I call indeed brahmans who do not hurt, kill, or cause the slaughter of any creatures, whether feeble or mighty.

24 (406) The ones I call indeed brahmans who are tolerant among the intolerant, mild among the violent, and free from greed among the greedy.

25 (407) The ones I call indeed brahmans from whom anger and hatred, pride and hypocrisy, have dropped like a mustard seed from the point of a needle.

26 (408) The ones I call indeed brahmans who utter true speech, instructive and free from harshness, so that they offend no one.

27 (409) The ones I call indeed brahmans who take nothing in the world that is not given them, be it long or short, small or large, good or bad.

13 Who foster no desires…: that is, who do not cling to some idea of what the next life might be like.

14 The other shore: nirvana. See ch. 2, n. 1.

15 Travel about without a home: that is, literally, live like a monk (specifically, a *bhikku* or homeless, wandering monk). The phrase may also be understood to mean: live without clinging to a notion of home, even if you do have a place where you eat, sleep, and work that could be labeled "home."

16 Free from all germs of renewed life: free from the cycle of birth, death, and rebirth (that is, enlightened and eligible for nirvana); also, free from even the tiniest elements that might blossom into desires.

28 (410) The ones I call indeed brahmans who foster no desires for this world or for the next[13]—who have no desires and are unshackled.

29 (411) The ones I call indeed brahmans who have no longings and, when they have understood the truth, do not express any doubt, and who have reached the depths of the eternal.

30 (412) The ones I call indeed brahmans who have risen in this world above bondage to both good and evil, who are free from grief, from sin, and from impurity.

31 (413) The ones I call indeed brahmans who are bright like the moon, pure, serene, and undisturbed—in whom all unseemly giddiness is extinct.

32 (414) The ones I call indeed brahmans who have traversed this miry road, the impossible world, difficult to travel, with all its vanities—who have gone across and reached the other shore,[14] who are thoughtful, steadfast, free from doubts, free from attachments, and content.

33 (415) The ones I call indeed brahmans who, having abandoned all desires in this world, travel about without a home[15]—and in whom covetousness is extinct.

34 (416) The ones I call indeed brahmans who, after leaving behind all attachments to others, have risen free from bondage to the gods.

35 (417) The ones I call indeed brahmans who have left what gives pleasure and what gives pain, who are cool in temperament and free from all germs of renewed life[16]—heroes who have conquered all the worlds.

36 (418) The ones I call indeed brahmans who know about the universal destruction and return of beings—and who are free from this bondage, joyful, and awakened.

17 Spiritual beings: *arahants* (Skt. *arhats*), those who have reached the pinnacle of Theravada training and have become spiritually enlightened. The path an *arahant* follows is unknown to the gods because they're too immersed in comfort and power; to the demons because they're too entrenched in misery; and to humans in general because they tend to be caught up in their own desires. According to Buddhist doctrine, the great advantage of having a human lifetime is that it alone gives one the opportunity to see the path, since a human being occupies "a middle way" between heaven (the gods) and hell (the demons). The motive for seeking the path is to end the particular kind of suffering one experiences as a human being.

18 The words "ahead," "behind," and "between" can be interpreted spatially (where things exist) or temporally (that is, "future," "past," and "present").

19 The Buddha saw his former lives in detail during the night of his enlightenment. Here the phrase doesn't necessarily imply such specific knowledge. Elsewhere the Buddha indicates that it is sufficient simply to know that one has had former lives.

20 The words "heaven and hell" are used collectively here to refer to countless heavenly and hellish domains in which one may languish during a given lifetime. They are not specific places of final judgment as in the Judeo-Christian sense of heaven or hell.

37 (419) The ones I call indeed brahmans whose path the gods do not know, nor do the demons, nor do humans in general—the ones whose desires are extinguished and who have become spiritual beings.[17]

38 (420) The ones I call indeed brahmans who call nothing their own, whether it be ahead, behind, or between[18]—who are poor and free from love of worldly things.

39 (421) The ones I call indeed brahmans who are valiant, noble, and heroic—the great sages, the conquerors, the sinless ones, the accomplished ones, the awakened ones.

40 (422) The ones I call indeed brahmans who know about their former lives,[19] who see heaven and hell,[20] who have reached the end of the cycle of births, who are perfect in knowledge, who are sages, and who have accomplished all that is to be accomplished.

Sources and Suggested Readings

Translations

Müller, Max. "The Dhammapada," in *Sacred Books of the East.* Oxford: Clarendon Press, 1870.

Babbitt, Irving. *The Dhammapada.* New York: Oxford University Press, 1936.

Burtt, E. A., ed. "Dhammapada," in *The Teachings of the Compassionate Buddha.* New York: New American Library, 1955.

Byrom, Thomas. *Dhammapada.* Boston: Shambhala, 1993.

Cleary, Thomas. *Dhammapada.* New York: Bantam, 1995.

Easwaran, Eknath. *The Dhammapada.* Petaluma, CA: Nilgiri Press, 1985.

Mascaró, Juan. *The Dhammapada.* New York: Penguin, 1973.

Rahula, Walpola. "Dhammapada," in *What the Buddha Taught.* New York: Grove Weidenfeld, 1959.

Warren, Henry Clarke. *Dhammapada.* New York: Atheneum, 1973.

Sources for Quotes and Suggested Readings on Buddhism

Armstrong, Karen. *Buddha.* New York: Viking Penguin, 2001.

Batchelor, Martine. *Meditation for Life.* Boston: Wisdom Publications, 2001.

Batchelor, Stephen. *Verses from the Center: A Buddhist Vision of the Sublime.* New York: Riverhead Books, 2000.

Bechert, Heinz, and Richard Gombrich. *The World of Buddhism.* London: Thames and Hudson, 1984.

Boisselier, Jean. *The Wisdom of the Buddha.* New York: Abrams, 1994.

Buddhadasa Bhikkhu. *Heartwood of the Bodhi Tree: The Buddha's Teaching on Voidness*. Boston: Wisdom Publications, 1994.

Chödrön, Pema. *When Things Fall Apart—Heart Advice For Difficult Times.* Boston: Shambhala Publications, Inc., 1997.

Cooper, David A. *Three Gates to Meditation Practice: A Personal Journey into Sufism, Buddhism, and Judaism.* Woodstock, Vt.: SkyLight Paths, 2000.

Dalai Lama, *The Path to Tranquility: Daily Meditations.* Ed. Renuka Singh. New York: Viking, 1999.

Harris, Elizabeth. *What Buddhists Believe.* Oxford: Oneworld Publications, 1998.

Khema, Ayya. *When the Iron Eagle Flies: Buddhism for the West.* Boston: Wisdom Publications, 2000.

Lowenstein, Tom. *The Vision of the Buddha.* Boston: Little, Brown, 1996.

Maguire, Jack. *Essential Buddhism.* New York: Simon & Schuster, 2001.

Maguire, Jack. *Waking Up: A Week Inside a Zen Monastery.* Woodstock, Vt.: SkyLight Paths, 2000.

McDonald, Kathleen. *How to Meditate: A Practical Guide.* Boston: Wisdom Publications, 1994.

Milarepa. *Drinking the Mountain Stream: Songs of Tibet's Beloved Saint, Milarepa.* Trans. Brian Cutillo. Boston: Wisdom Publications, 1995.

Nelson, Marcia Z. *Come and Sit: A Week Inside Meditation Centers.* Woodstock, Vt.: SkyLight Paths, 2001.

Nhat Hanh, Thich. *Being Peace.* Berkeley, Calif.: Parallax Press, 1996.

Nhat Hanh, Thich, and Fred Eppsteiner. *Interbeing: Fourteen Guidelines for Engaged Buddhism.* Berkeley, Calif.: Parallax Press, 1993.

Nhat Hanh, Thich, and Nguyen T. Hop. *Old Path White Clouds: Walking in the Footsteps of the Buddha.* Berkeley, Calif.: Parallax Press, 1991.

Pauling, Chris. *Introducing Buddhism.* Birmingham: Windhorse, 1990.

Rinpoche, Lama Zopa. *The Door to Satisfaction: The Heart Advice of a Tibetan Buddhist Master.* Boston: Wisdom Publications, 1994.

Sanders, Kenneth. *Wisdom of the East.* Oxford: Clarendon Press, 1889.

Snelling, John. *The Elements of Buddhism.* Longmead: Element Books, 1990.

Surya Das, Lama. *Awakening the Buddha Within: Tibetan Wisdom for the Western World.* New York: Broadway Books, 1997.

Thurman, Robert A. F. *Inner Revolution: Life, Liberty, and the Pursuit of Real Happiness.* New York: Riverhead Books, 1998.

Yeshe, Lama Thubten. *The Bliss of Inner Fire: Heart Practice of the Six Yogas of Naropa.* Boston: Wisdom Publications, 1998.

List of Special Terms

Below are brief definitions and explanations of selected terms in Pali, Sanskrit, and English found in the text and annotations. They are indexed here by page numbers and note numbers (i.e., 9, n. 1 = page 9, note 1), directing you to the full definition or explanation of each term in the book. If both the Pali and Sanskrit terms are given, each language is indicated in parentheses.

arahant (Pali), enlightened one, 30, n. 1
arhat (Skt.), enlightened one, 30, n. 1
ariya (Pali), noble or elect one, 8, n. 2
arya (Skt.), noble or elect one, 8, n. 2
bhikku (Pali), wandering monk, 10, n. 6; 110, n. 1
bhikkuni (Pali), wandering nun, 110, n. 1
bhikshu (Skt.), wandering monk, 10, n. 6; 110, n. 1
bhikshuni (Skt.), wandering nun, 110, n. 1
bodhisattva, enlightened being who helps others, 30, n. 1
Brahma, the creator, 34, n. 3
brahman (brahmin), priest, member of the highest Hindu caste, 44, n. 8
buddha, awakened one, 58, n. 1
cycle of birth, death, and rebirth, see *samsara*
desire (three types of), 102, n. 1
dhamma (Pali), dharma, 2, n. 3
dhammapada, xix
Dhanapalaka, mythic elephant, 98, n. 3
dharma (Skt.), universal law or truth, the way, 2, n. 3
Dharma (Skt.), the Buddha's teachings, 2, n. 3 (see also Three Jewels)
duhkha (Skt.), suffering, 62, n. 1
dukkha (Pali), suffering, 62, n. 1
Four Noble Truths, 60, n. 8
full moon, symbol of enlightenment, 54, n. 3
Gautama (Skt.), name of the Buddha, xx
gods, 4, n. 6; 10, n. 5; 30, n. 5
Gotama (Pali), name of the Buddha, xx
hell, 4, n. 6; 94, n. 1, n. 2, n. 4
Indra, king of gods, 10, n. 5
infinite void, see *sunnata/shunyata*
kamma (Pali), karma, 22, n. 5
karma (Skt.), law of cause and effect, 22, n. 5
khanda (Pali), five impermanent aggregates, 46, n. 2
knowledge (seven elements of), 28, n. 7
Law/law, see Dharma and dharma
lotus, symbol of the inner perfection of each human being, 102, n. 3
Maghavan, king of gods, 10, n. 5

Mahayana, vehicle of Buddhism, xix; 30, n. 1
Mara, evil tempter, 2, n. 4
merit, 36, n. 6
middle way, 22, n. 4; 94, n. 5
nama-rupa, name and form, 70, n. 1
name and form, see *nama-rupa*
nibbana (Pali), nirvana, 8, n. 1; 88, n. 16
nirvana (Skt.), 8, n. 1; 88, n. 16
Noble Eightfold Path, 60, n. 8
precepts, Buddhist vows, 54, n. 6
rebirth, 4, n. 6; 30, n. 1; 40, n. 4
samana (Pali), contemplative ascetic, 82, n. 7
samkhara (Pali), phenomenon made up of five aggregates, 86, n. 7
samsara (Pali, Skt.), cycle of birth, death, and rebirth, 8, n. 1; 28, n. 5
samskara (Skt.), karma-created patterns, 38, n. 1
sangha/Sangha, community of the Buddha's followers, 60, n. 7
sankhara (Pali), karma-created patterns, 38, n. 1
shamana (Skt.), contemplative ascetic, 82, n. 7
shunyata (Skt.), infinite void, 30, n. 2
Siddhatta (Pali), name of the Buddha, xx
Siddhartha (Skt.), name of the Buddha, xx
sin (three forms of), 72, n. 5
skandha (Skt.), five impermanent aggregates, 46, n. 2
Sugata, Happy One (epithet for the Buddha), 88, n. 15
suhkha (Skt.), happiness, 62, n. 1
sukkha (Pali), happiness, 62, n. 1
sunnata (Pali), infinite void, 30, n. 2
tanha (Pali), thirst (desire), 102, n. 1
tathagata, enlightened one, 78, n. 10
Tathagata, epithet for the Buddha, 78, n. 10
"ten thousand things," all phenomena, 34, n. 1
thera, elder, 80, n. 4
Theravada, vehicle of Buddhism, xix; 30, n. 1 (also see *thera*)
"thirty-six channels," all types of sensual experiences, 102, n. 5
Three Jewels, the Buddha, Dharma, and Sangha, 60, n. 7
trishna (Skt.), thirst (desire), 102, n. 1
Vajrayana, vehicle of Buddhism, xix; 30, n. 1
vehicle (Buddhist), xix
worlds/realms of being, 4, n. 6
Yama, Hindu god of death, 16, n. 2

out SKYLIGHT PATHS Publishing

ht Paths Publishing is creating a place where people of different al traditions come together for challenge and inspiration, a place we can help each other understand the mystery that lies at the heart existence.

h spirituality, our religious beliefs are increasingly becoming a part ives—rather than *apart* from our lives. While many of us may be erested than ever in spiritual growth, we may be less firmly planted in traditional religion. Yet, we do want to deepen our relationship to the sacred, to learn from our own as well as from other faith traditions, and to practice in new ways.

SkyLight Paths sees both believers and seekers as a community that increasingly transcends traditional boundaries of religion and denomination—people wanting to learn from each other, *walking together, finding the way.*

We at SkyLight Paths take great care to produce beautiful books that present meaningful spiritual content in a form that reflects the art of making high quality books. Therefore, we want to acknowledge those who contributed to the production of this book.

PRODUCTION
Tim Holtz & Bridgett Taylor

EDITORIAL
Amanda Dupuis, Martha McKinney,
Polly Short Mahoney & Emily Wichland

COVER DESIGN
Walter C. Bumford III, Stockton, Massachusetts

TEXT DESIGN
Chelsea Cloeter, Scotia, New York

PRINTING AND BINDING
Versa Press, East Peoria, Illinois

AVAILABLE FROM BETTER BOOKSTORES.
TRY YOUR BOOKSTORE FIRST.

Other Interesting Books—Spirituality

Lighting the Lamp of Wisdom: *A Week Inside a Yoga Ashram*

by *John Ittner;* Foreword by *Dr. David Frawley*

This insider's guide to Hindu spiritual life takes you into a typical week of retreat inside a yoga ashram to demystify the experience and show you what to expect from your own visit. Includes a discussion of worship services, meditation and yoga classes, chanting and music, work practice, and more.

6 x 9, 192 pp, b/w photographs, Quality PB, ISBN 1-893361-52-7 **$15.95**;
HC, ISBN 1-893361-37-3 **$24.95**

Waking Up: *A Week Inside a Zen Monastery*

by *Jack Maguire;* Foreword by *John Daido Loori, Roshi*

An essential guide to what it's like to spend a week inside a Zen Buddhist monastery.

6 x 9, 224 pp, b/w photographs, Quality PB, ISBN 1-893361-55-1 **$16.95**;
HC, ISBN 1-893361-13-6 **$21.95**

Making a Heart for God: *A Week Inside a Catholic Monastery*

by *Dianne Aprile;* Foreword by *Brother Patrick Hart,* OCSO

This essential guide to experiencing life in a Catholic monastery takes you to the Abbey of Gethsemani—the Trappist monastery in Kentucky that was home to author Thomas Merton—to explore the details. "More balanced and informative than the popular *The Cloister Walk* by Kathleen Norris." —*Choice: Current Reviews for Academic Libraries*

6 x 9, 224 pp, b/w photographs, Quality PB, ISBN 1-893361-49-7 **$16.95**;
HC, ISBN 1-893361-14-4 **$21.95**

Come and Sit: *A Week Inside Meditation Centers*

by *Marcia Z. Nelson;* Foreword by *Wayne Teasdale*

The insider's guide to meditation in a variety of different spiritual traditions. Traveling through Buddhist, Hindu, Christian, Jewish, and Sufi traditions, this essential guide takes you to different meditation centers to meet the teachers and students and learn about the practices, demystifying the meditation experience.

6 x 9, 224 pp, b/w photographs, Quality PB, ISBN 1-893361-35-7 **$16.95**

Or phone, fax, mail or e-mail to: SKYLIGHT PATHS **Publishing**
Sunset Farm Offices, Route 4 • P.O. Box 237 • Woodstock, Vermont 05091
Tel: (802) 457-4000 • Fax: (802) 457-4004 • www.skylightpaths.com
Credit card orders: (800) 962-4544 (8:30AM–5:30PM ET Monday–Friday)

Generous discounts on quantity orders. SATISFACTION GUARANTEED. Prices subject to change.

Spirituality

Who Is My God?
An Innovative Guide to Finding Your Spiritual Identity

Created by *the Editors at SkyLight Paths*

Spiritual Type™ + Tradition Indicator = Spiritual Identity

Your Spiritual Identity is an undeniable part of who you are—whether you've thought much about it or not. This dynamic resource provides a helpful framework to begin or deepen your spiritual growth. Start by taking the unique Spiritual Identity Self-Test™; tabulate your results; then explore one, two or more of twenty-eight faiths/spiritual paths followed in America today. "An innovative and entertaining way to think—and rethink—about your own spiritual path, or perhaps even to find one." —Dan Wakefield, author of *How Do We Know When It's God?*
6 x 9, 160 pp, Quality PB Original, ISBN 1-893361-08-X **$15.95**

Spiritual Manifestos: *Visions for Renewed Religious Life in America from Young Spiritual Leaders of Many Faiths*

Edited by *Niles Elliot Goldstein;* Preface by *Martin E. Marty*

Discover the reasons why so many people have kept organized religion at arm's length.

Here, ten young spiritual leaders, most in their mid-thirties, representing the spectrum of religious traditions—Protestant, Catholic, Jewish, Buddhist, Unitarian Universalist—present the innovative ways they are transforming our spiritual communities and our lives. "These ten articulate young spiritual leaders engender hope for the vitality of 21st-century religion." —Forrest Church, Minister of All Souls Church in New York City
6 x 9, 256 pp, HC, ISBN 1-893361-09-8 **$21.95**

Jewish Spirituality: *A Brief Introduction for Christians*

by *Lawrence Kushner*

Lawrence Kushner, whose award-winning books have brought Jewish spirituality to life for countless readers of all faiths and backgrounds, tailors his unique style to address Christian's questions, revealing the essence of Judaism in a way that people whose own tradition traces its roots to Judaism can understand and enjoy.
5½ x 8½, 112 pp, Quality PB Original, ISBN 1-58023-150-0 **$12.95**

The Geography of Faith
Underground Conversations on Religious, Political and Social Change

by *Daniel Berrigan* and *Robert Coles;* Updated introduction and afterword by the authors

A classic of faith-based activism—updated for a new generation.

Listen in on the conversations between these two great teachers—one a renegade priest wanted by the FBI for his protests against the Vietnam war, the other a future Pulitzer Prize-winning journalist—as they struggle with what it means to put your faith to the test. Discover how their story of challenging the status quo during a time of great political, religious, and social change is just as applicable to our lives today. 6 x 9, 224 pp, Quality PB, ISBN 1-893361-40-3 **$16.95**

Spirituality

Inspired Lives: *Exploring the Role of Faith and Spirituality in the Lives of Extraordinary People*
by *Joanna Laufer* and *Kenneth S. Lewis*
Contributors include *Ang Lee, Wynton Marsalis, Kathleen Norris,* and many more

How faith transforms the lives and work of the creative and innovative people in our world.

In this moving book, soul-searching conversations unearth the importance of spirituality and personal faith for more than forty artists and innovators who have made a real difference in our world through their work. 6 x 9, 256 pp, Quality PB, ISBN 1-893361-33-0 **$16.95**

Women Pray
Voices through the Ages, from Many Faiths, Cultures, and Traditions
Edited and with introductions by *Monica Furlong*

Many ways—new and old—to communicate with the Divine.

This beautiful gift book celebrates the rich variety of ways women around the world have called out to the Divine—with words of joy, praise, gratitude, wonder, petition, longing, and even anger—from the ancient world up to our own time. Prayers from women of nearly every religious or spiritual background give us an eloquent expression of what it means to communicate with God. 5 x 7¼, 256 pp, Deluxe HC with ribbon marker, ISBN 1-893361-25-X **$19.95**

Zen Effects: *The Life of Alan Watts*
by *Monica Furlong*

The first and only full-length biography of one of the most charismatic spiritual leaders of the twentieth century—now back in print!

Through his widely popular books and lectures, Alan Watts (1915–1973) did more to introduce Eastern philosophy and religion to Western minds than any figure before or since. Here is the only biography of this charismatic figure, who served as Zen teacher, Anglican priest, lecturer, academic, entertainer, a leader of the San Francisco renaissance, and author of more than 30 books, including *The Way of Zen, Psychotherapy East and West* and *The Spirit of Zen.*
6 x 9, 264 pp, Quality PB, ISBN 1-893361-32-2 **$16.95**

Simone Weil: *A Modern Pilgrimage*
by *Robert Coles*

The extraordinary life of the spiritual philosopher who's been called both saint and madwoman.

The French writer and philosopher Simone Weil (1906–1943) devoted her life to a search for God—while avoiding membership in organized religion. Robert Coles' intriguing study of Weil details her short, eventful life, and is an insightful portrait of the beloved and controversial thinker whose life and writings influenced many (from T. S. Eliot to Adrienne Rich to Albert Camus), and continue to inspire seekers everywhere. 6 x 9, 208 pp, Quality PB, ISBN 1-893361-34-9 **$16.95**

Spirituality

Three Gates to Meditation Practice
A Personal Journey into Sufism, Buddhism, and Judaism

by *David A. Cooper*

Shows us how practicing within more than one spiritual tradition can lead us to our true home.

Here are over fifteen years from the journey of "post-denominational rabbi" David A. Cooper, author of *God Is a Verb,* and his wife, Shoshana—years in which the Coopers explored a rich variety of practices, from chanting Sufi *dhikr* to Buddhist Vipassana meditation, to the study of kabbalah and esoteric Judaism. Their experience demonstrates that the spiritual path is really completely within our reach, whoever we are, whatever we do—as long as we are willing to practice it. 5½ x 8½, 240 pp, Quality PB, ISBN 1-893361-22-5 **$16.95**

Praying with Our Hands: *Twenty-One Practices of Embodied Prayer from the World's Spiritual Traditions*

by *Jon M. Sweeney;* Photographs by *Jennifer J. Wilson;*
Foreword by *Mother Tessa Bielecki;* Afterword by *Taitetsu Unno, Ph.D.*

A spiritual guidebook for bringing prayer into our bodies.

This inspiring book of reflections and accompanying photographs shows us twenty-one simple ways of using our hands to speak to God, to enrich our devotion and ritual. All express the various approaches of the world's religious traditions to bringing the body into worship. Spiritual traditions represented include Anglican, Sufi, Zen, Roman Catholic, Yoga, Shaker, Hindu, Jewish, Pentecostal, Eastern Orthodox, and many others.
8 x 8, 96 pp, 22 duotone photographs, Quality PB Original, ISBN 1-893361-16-0 **$16.95**

The Sacred Art of Listening
Forty Reflections for Cultivating a Spiritual Practice

by *Kay Lindahl;* Illustrations by *Amy Schnapper*

More than ever before, we need to embrace the skills and practice of listening. You will learn to: Speak clearly from your heart • Communicate with courage and compassion • Heighten your awareness for deep listening • Enhance your ability to listen to people with different belief systems. 8 x 8, 160 pp, Illus., Quality PB Original, ISBN 1-893361-44-6 **$16.95**

Labyrinths from the Outside In
Walking to Spiritual Insight—a Beginner's Guide

by *Donna Schaper* and *Carole Ann Camp*

The user-friendly, interfaith guide to making and using labyrinths—for meditation, prayer, and celebration.

Labyrinth walking is a spiritual exercise *anyone* can do. This accessible guide unlocks the mysteries of the labyrinth for all of us, providing ideas for using the labyrinth walk for prayer, meditation, and celebrations to mark the most important moments in life. Includes instructions for making a labyrinth of your own and finding one in your area.
6 x 9, 208 pp, b/w illus. and photographs, Quality PB Original, ISBN 1-893361-18-7 **$16.95**

SkyLight Illuminations Series

Andrew Harvey, series editor

Offers today's spiritual seeker an enjoyable entry into the great classic texts of the world's spiritual traditions. Each classic is presented in an accessible translation, with facing pages of guided commentary from experts, giving you the keys you need to understand the history, context, and meaning of the text. This series enables readers of all backgrounds to experience and understand classic spiritual texts directly, and to make them a part of their lives. Andrew Harvey writes the foreword to each volume, an insightful, personal introduction to each classic.

Hasidic Tales: *Annotated & Explained*

Translation and annotation by *Rabbi Rami Shapiro*

The legendary tales of the impassioned Hasidic rabbis.

The allegorical quality of Hasidic tales can be perplexing. Here, they are presented as stories rather than parables, making them accessible and meaningful. Each demonstrates the spiritual power of unabashed joy, offers lessons for leading a holy life, and reminds us that the Divine can be found in the everyday. Annotations explain theological concepts, introduce major characters, and clarify references unfamiliar to most readers.
5½ x 8½, 240 pp, Quality PB, ISBN 1-893361-86-1 **$16.95**

Bhagavad Gita: *Annotated & Explained*

Translation by *Shri Purohit Swami;* Annotation by *Kendra Crossen Burroughs*

"The very best Gita for first-time readers." —Ken Wilber

Millions of people turn daily to India's most beloved holy book, whose universal appeal has made it popular with non-Hindus and Hindus alike. This SkyLight Illuminations edition of the Gita introduces readers to the characters; explains references and philosophical terms; shares the interpretations of famous spiritual leaders and scholars; and more.
5½ x 8½, 208 pp, Quality PB, ISBN 1-893361-28-4 **$15.95**

The Gospel of Thomas: *Annotated & Explained*

Translation and annotation by *Stevan Davies*

Discovered in 1945, this collection of aphoristic sayings sheds new light on the origins of Christianity and the intriguing figure of Jesus, portraying the Kingdom of God as a present fact about the world, rather than a future promise or future threat. This edition guides you through the text with annotations that focus on the meaning of the sayings.
5½ x 8½, 192 pp, Quality PB, ISBN 1-893361-45-4 **$16.95**

Spirituality

Honey from the Rock
An Introduction to Jewish Mysticism

by *Lawrence Kushner*

An insightful and absorbing introduction to the ten gates of Jewish mysticism and how it applies to daily life. "The easiest introduction to Jewish mysticism you can read."

6 x 9, 176 pp, Quality PB, ISBN 1-58023-073-3 **$15.95**

Eyes Remade for Wonder
The Way of Jewish Mysticism and Sacred Living

A Lawrence Kushner Reader

Intro. by *Thomas Moore*, author of *Care of the Soul*

Whether you are new to Kushner or a devoted fan, you'll find inspiration here. With samplings from each of Kushner's works, and a generous amount of new material, this book is to be read and reread, each time discovering deeper layers of meaning in our lives.

6 x 9, 240 pp, Quality PB, ISBN 1-58023-042-3 **$16.95**; HC, ISBN 1-58023-014-8 **$23.95**

Invisible Lines of Connection
Sacred Stories of the Ordinary

by *Lawrence Kushner* AWARD WINNER!

Through his everyday encounters with family, friends, colleagues and strangers, Kushner takes us deeply into our lives, finding flashes of spiritual insight in the process.

5½ x 8½, 160 pp, Quality PB, ISBN 1-879045-98-2 **$15.95**; HC, ISBN 1-879045-52-4 **$21.95**

One God Clapping: *The Spiritual Path of a Zen Rabbi*

by *Alan Lew* with *Sherril Jaffe*

Firsthand account of a spiritual journey from Zen Buddhist practitioner to rabbi.

A fascinating personal story of a Jewish meditation expert's roundabout spiritual journey from Zen Buddhist practitioner to rabbi. An insightful source of inspiration for each of us who is on the journey to find God in today's multi-faceted spiritual world.

5½ x 8½, 336 pp, Quality PB, ISBN 1-58023-115-2 **$16.95**

A Heart of Stillness
A Complete Guide to Learning the Art of Meditation

by *David A. Cooper*

The only complete, nonsectarian guide to meditation, from one of our most respected spiritual teachers.

Experience what mystics have experienced for thousands of years. *A Heart of Stillness* helps you acquire on your own, with minimal guidance, the skills of various styles of meditation. Draws upon the wisdom teachings of Christianity, Judaism, Buddhism, Hinduism, and Islam as it teaches you the processes of purification, concentration, and mastery in detail.

5½ x 8½, 272 pp, Quality PB, ISBN 1-893361-03-9 **$16.95**

Books in the "Perfect Stranger" Series

How to Be a Perfect Stranger, In 2 Volumes
A Guide to Etiquette in Other People's Religious Ceremonies

Ed. by *Stuart M. Matlins* and *Arthur J. Magida* **AWARD WINNERS!**

Explains the rituals and celebrations of North America's major religions/denominations, helping an interested guest to feel comfortable, participate to the fullest extent possible, and avoid violating anyone's religious principles. Answers practical questions from the perspective of *any* other faith.

Vol. 1: North America's Largest Faiths

VOL. 1 COVERS: Assemblies of God • Baptist • Buddhist • Christian Church (Disciples of Christ) • Christian Science • Churches of Christ • Episcopalian/Anglican • Greek Orthodox • Hindu • Islam • Jehovah's Witnesses • Jewish • Lutheran • Methodist • Mormon • Presbyterian • Quaker • Roman Catholic • Seventh-day Adventist • United Church of Canada • United Church of Christ 6 x 9, 432 pp, Quality PB, ISBN 1-893361-01-2 **$19.95**

Vol. 2: More Faiths in North America

VOL. 2 COVERS: African American Methodist Churches • Baha'i • Christian and Missionary Alliance • Christian Congregation • Church of the Brethren • Church of the Nazarene • Evangelical Free Church • International Church of the Foursquare Gospel • International Pentecostal Holiness Church • Mennonite/Amish • Native American/First Nations • Orthodox Churches • Pentecostal Church of God • Reformed Church • Sikh • Unitarian Universalist • Wesleyan 6 x 9, 416 pp, Quality PB, ISBN 1-893361-02-0 **$19.95**

The Perfect Stranger's Guide to Funerals and Grieving Practices
A Guide to Etiquette in Other People's Religious Ceremonies

Edited by *Stuart M. Matlins*

6 x 9, 240 pp, Quality PB, ISBN 1-893361-20-9 **$16.95**

The Perfect Stranger's Guide to Wedding Ceremonies
A Guide to Etiquette in Other People's Religious Ceremonies

Edited by *Stuart M. Matlins*

6 x 9, 208 pp, Quality PB, ISBN 1-893361-19-5 **$16.95**

AVAILABLE FROM BETTER BOOKSTORES.
TRY YOUR BOOKSTORE FIRST.

Other Interesting Books—Spirituality

God Within: *Our Spiritual Future—As Told by Today's New Adults*

Edited by *Jon M. Sweeney* and *the Editors at SkyLight Paths*

Our faith, in our words.

The future of spirituality in America lies in the vision of the women and men who are the children of the "baby boomer" generation—born into the post-New-Age world of the 1970s and 1980s. This book gives voice to their spiritual energy, and allows readers of all ages to share in their passionate quests for faith and belief. Sometimes irreverent—but always *relevant*—this thought-provoking collection of writings, poetry, and art showcases the voices that are defining the future of religion, faith, and belief as we know it.

6 x 9, 176 pp, Quality PB Original, ISBN 1-893361-15-2 **$14.95**

Releasing the Creative Spirit: *Unleash the Creativity in Your Life*

by *Dan Wakefield*

From the author of *How Do We Know When It's God?*—
a practical guide to accessing creative power in every area of your life.

In this passionate, personal guide, award-winning author Dan Wakefield explodes the myths associated with the creative process and shows how everyone can uncover and develop their natural ability to create. Drawing on religion, psychology, and the arts, he teaches us that the key to creation of any kind is clarity—of body, mind, and spirit—and he provides practical exercises that each of us can do to access that centered quality that allows creativity to shine.

7 x 10, 208 pp, Quality PB, ISBN 1-893361-36-5 **$16.95**

The Gospel of Thomas: *A Guidebook for Spiritual Practice*

by *Ron Miller;* Translations by *Stevan Davies*

An innovative guide to bring a new spiritual classic into daily life.

This unique guidebook offers you a way to translate the wisdom of the Gospel of Thomas into daily practice, manifesting in your life the same consciousness revealed in Jesus of Nazareth. Written for readers of all religious backgrounds, this guidebook will help you to apply Jesus's wisdom to your own life and to the world around you.

6 x 9, 160 pp, Quality PB Original, ISBN 1-59473-047-4 **$14.99**

Or phone, fax, mail or e-mail to: SKYLIGHT PATHS **Publishing**
Sunset Farm Offices, Route 4 • P.O. Box 237 • Woodstock, Vermont 05091
Tel: (802) 457-4000 • Fax: (802) 457-4004 • www.skylightpaths.com
Credit card orders: **(800) 962-4544** (9AM–5PM ET Monday–Friday)

Generous discounts on quantity orders. Satisfaction guaranteed. Prices subject to change.